# THE WORLD CHANGERS

## TOP 100 POLITICAL LEADERS OF ALL TIME

SAVITA PANDIT



TRUE SIGN
PUBLISHING HOUSE

**Published by True Sign Publishing House**
Address: 21, 2nd Floor, Kundan Nagar, Bagmugaliya,
Bhopal, Madhya Pradesh - 462026
E-mail: truesignbooks@gmail.com
Website: www.truesign.in



**The World Changers**
**Top 100 Political Leaders Of All Time**

**Author:** Savita Pandit

ISBN: 978-93-5988-184-3

First Edition: 2023

---



---

# CONTENTS

# 1.

# WINSTON CHURCHILL (UK)

The British politician, orator, and writer Winston Churchill was born on November 30, 1874, at Blenheim Palace, Oxfordshire, England, and died in London on January 24, 1965. He served as prime minister from 1940 to 1945 and from 1951 to 1955, and he rallied the British people and led his country to victory in World War II.

Despite his meteoric ascent to national political prominence political political prominence leading up to World War I, Churchill became notorious for his unpredictable decision-making throughout the conflict and the following decade. Due to his dubious political standing, he lived a solitary life until 1940, when he rose to the position of national coalition leader in response to Adolf Hitler's challenge. After shaping Allied policy in WWII with FDR and Stalin, he warned the West of the Soviet Union's expansionist menace after the alliance broke apart. In 1951, he successfully re-elected the Conservative Party to government and continued in that role until his departure due to illness in 1955.

The English-speaking peoples, whose unity he would relentlessly seek to foster in times of peace and conflict, were in Churchill's veins. He was directly derived from the early 18th-century hero John Churchill, 1st Duke of Marlborough, who fought against Louis XIV of France, via his father, the soaring Tory politician Lord Randolph Churchill. His mother, Jennie Jerome, was the daughter of Leonard W. Jerome, a wealthy New Yorker and a huge horse racing fan.

Only the love and care of his dedicated nurse, Mrs. Everest, saved the young Churchill from a troubled and neglected infancy. His academically dismal performance at Harrow gave the impression that his father had been right to enlist him in the military. He took the admission test to the "Royal Military College", now the "Academy at Sandhurst", three times before he finally succeeded. However, he worked very hard while he was there and graduated twenty-first out of one hundred thirty. He enlisted in the 4th Hussars in 1895, the same year his father died tragically. While on leave for a few months, he covered the Cuban revolution against Spain for the Daily Graphic (London), his only opportunity for action at the time. Serving in the North-West Frontier in India as a soldier and writer in 1896, he was a member of his regiment (1897). His dispatches, later expanded as "The Story of the Malakand Field Force (1898)", were so well-received that they set him on the path to a lifelong sporadic publishing. While serving as a soldier and journalist for Lord Kitchener's Nile campaign army in 1897 and 1898, he penned Savrola (1900), a romance book set in Ruritanian England. An excellent account of the conflict is found in The River War (1899).

# 2.

# NELSON MANDELA (SOUTH AFRICA)

Born on July 18, 1918, in Mvezo, South Africa, Nelson Mandela was the first "Black president of South Africa" (1994–1999) and a Black nationalist. He died on December 5, 2013, in Johannesburg. He was instrumental in ending racial segregation and bringing about a peaceful transition towards majority rule in South Africa during his discussions with President F.W. de Klerk in the early 1990s. In 1993, Mandela and de Klerk shared the Nobel Peace Prize.

The chief of the Xhosa-speaking Tembu people, Henry Mandela, was Nelson Mandela's father. After his father passed away, Jongintaba, the regent of the Tembu, took it upon himself to nurture young Nelson. Nelson decided to become a lawyer instead of claiming chieftainship. He became a lawyer after attending South African Native College (now known as the University of Fort Hare) and the University of the Witwatersrand, where he studied law and passed the qualifying test. He became a leader in the African National Congress's (ANC) Youth League after joining the Black Liberation Organization in

1944. He wed Evelyn Ntoko Mase the same year they met. After that, Mandela moved on to other leadership roles within the ANC, where he reenergized the group and continued to fight against the National Party's apartheid policies.

To handle matters stemming from apartheid laws enacted after 1948, Mandela and fellow ANC leader Oliver Tambo founded the first Black legal practice in South Africa in Johannesburg in 1952. Mandela was also instrumental in that year's uprising against South Africa's pass laws, which mandated that nonwhites have official documentation (passbooks, reference books, etc.) proving their right to be in what the government considered "restricted" areas—those typically inhabited by white people. He went on a cross-country tour as part of the campaign, rallying people behind peaceful resistance to the discriminatory legislation. He helped write the Freedom Charter, which demanded social democracy in South Africa free from racial discrimination, in 1955.

The government often targeted Mandela because of his antiapartheid activity. Intermittent bans (severe restrictions on travel, affiliation, and speech) began against him in 1952. The purpose of his arrest in December 1956, along with over a hundred others, was to apprehend antiapartheid activists by use of treason accusations. In 1961, Mandela was finally freed after trial that same year. Nomzamo Winifred Madikizela (Winnie Madikizela-Mandela) was his bride during the protracted legal processes that resulted in his first wife's divorce.

# 3.

# MAHATMA GANDHI (INDIA)

Mahatma Gandhi, also known as Mohandas Karamchand Gandhi, was born on October 2, 1869, in Porbandar, India. He passed away on January 30, 1948, in Delhi. Gandhi was a prominent figure in Indian nationalism and a renowned advocate for nonviolence throughout the 20th century. Gandhi was raised in a household deeply immersed in religion, where he naturally embraced religious tolerance and the principle of ahimsa (nonviolence towards all sentient creatures). He pursued a legal degree in England from 1888 to 1891 and then secured employment with an Indian company in South Africa in 1893. He emerged as a proficient champion for the rights of the Indian community.

In 1906, he first used satyagraha, his method of peaceful opposition. His triumph in South Africa bestowed upon him global renown, and in 1915, he repatriated to India and swiftly ascended to the position of the foremost advocate for Indian self-governance, leading a statewide campaign. By 1920, Gandhi had achieved unprecedented power that no other political leader in India had ever acquired.

Gandhi transformed the Indian National Congress into a potent political tool for Indian nationalism and led significant nonviolent resistance movements throughout 1920–22, 1930–34 (including his historic march to the sea to protest a government monopoly on salt), and 1940–42. In the 1930s, he actively advocated for the cessation of prejudice against India's lower-caste "untouchables" (Dalits; formally recognised as Scheduled Castes) and focused on providing education to rural areas of India and encouraging the development of cottage industries.

In 1947, India attained dominion status. However, the partition of the subcontinent into Pakistan and India was a profound disappointment to Gandhi, who had dedicated considerable efforts towards fostering Hindu-Muslim cooperation. In September 1947, he quelled the riots in Calcutta (Kolkata) via a period of fasting. Gandhi, often known as the Mahatma ("Great-Souled"), had garnered the love and devotion of millions. In January 1948, he was assassinated by a young Hindu extremist.

Gandhi was the youngest age during his father's marriage. Karamchand Gandhi, the father of the individual in question, held the position of dewan (chief minister) in Porbandar, the capital of a tiny principality in western India, under British suzerainty. Karamchand Gandhi did not get a substantial formal education despite his influential position. Nevertheless, he was a competent administrator who adeptly navigated the unpredictable princes, their patient people, and the assertive British political officials in authority.

Putlibai, Gandhi's mother, was deeply devoted to religion, indifferent to material possessions or adornments, and dedicated her time to her household and the temple. She routinely observed fasting and tirelessly cared for her family during illness. Mohandas was raised in a household deeply immersed in Vaishnavism, a form of Hinduism centered on worshipping the deity Vishnu. The household also significantly influenced Jainism, an Indian religion known for its strict moral principles, including nonviolence and the belief in the eternal nature of everything in the world. Consequently, he unquestioningly embraced the principles of ahimsa (avoiding harm to all living creatures), vegetarianism, self-purification via fasting, and mutual tolerance among followers of different beliefs and factions.

# 4.

# FRANKLIN D. ROOSEVELT (USA)

Born in 1882, which is now a national historic landmark in Hyde Park, New York, he went to Harvard and Columbia Law. Eleanor Roosevelt was his bride. They tied the knot on St. Patrick's Day, 1905. Franklin D. Roosevelt followed in the footsteps of his revered fifth cousin, President Theodore Roosevelt, and became involved in politics, although as a Democrat, to serve the public. In 1910, he was elected to the Senate of New York.

In 1920, he was nominated for vice president by the Democrats and was named assistant secretary of the navy by President Wilson.

Tragically, he had poliomyelitis in the summer of 1921 at the age of 39. He battled valiantly to recover the use of his legs, especially via swimming, displaying unwavering bravery. He made a remarkable comeback at the 1924 Democratic Convention, using crutches to propose Alfred E. Smith as "the Happy Warrior." Roosevelt assumed the office of New York governor in 1928.

In November 1932, he was elected to the first of his four terms as president. Nearly every bank had closed its doors by March, and thirteen million people were unemployed. Within his first "hundred days" in office, he advocated for, and Congress passed, a comprehensive programme to revive the economy, protect homeowners and farmers from foreclosure, provide jobs for the jobless, and reform the system, notably by establishing the Tennessee Valley Authority.

Although the economy had begun to show signs of improvement by 1935, business leaders and bankers were increasingly opposed to Roosevelt's New Deal agenda. People despised the labour concessions, were terrified of his experiments, and were outraged that he had decoupled the country from the gold standard permitted fiscal deficits. In response, Roosevelt unveiled a new reform agenda that included Social Security, more taxes on the rich, tighter regulation of financial institutions and public utilities, and a massive job assistance programme for the jobless.

A lopsided majority of voters re-elected him in 1936. The Supreme Court had been striking down important New Deal policies, so Roosevelt felt he had the people's support and wanted to expand it. Even if Roosevelt lost the struggle with the Supreme Court, a constitutional law revolution occurred. The government would then be able to lawfully control the economy.

By pledging American support for the "good neighbour" approach, Roosevelt turned the Monroe Doctrine into a plan for joint defence against aggressors, shifting it from a unilateral American credo. In addition to trying to empower countries that were threatened or attacked, he wanted to keep the US out of the European conflict via neutrality laws. In 1940, when England was besieged and France collapsed, he sent Great Britain all the help he could think of, avoiding direct military action.

The Japanese bombed Pearl Harbour on December 7, 1941, and President Roosevelt immediately ordered the mobilisation of American forces for war.

His deep concern for the future of global peace drove him to dedicate much time and energy to establishing a United Nations, where he believed international conflicts might be resolved.

In the latter days of the war, Roosevelt's health began to fail, and he passed away from a brain haemorrhage on April 12, 1945, in Warm Springs, Georgia.

# 5.

# CLEOPATRA (EGYPT)

Things were not going according to plan for Cleopatra VII in her conflict with her younger brother for the Egyptian throne. Cleopatra tried to establish herself as the sole ruler in 49 B.C. However, her sister was expelled from the palace at Alexandria by her husband, Ptolemy XIII, who was also her co-ruler, according to their father's will. Having escaped to Syria while she was in her early twenties, the queen eventually returned with a mercenary army and camped outside the city.

As Julius Caesar, a Roman commander, arrived in Alexandria in the summer of 48 B.C. to pursue a military opponent who had fled to Egypt, he became entangled in the Egyptian family rivalry. Rome had long relied on Egypt as an obedient friend, and the Nile Valley's continued prosperity as an agricultural hub was in Rome's financial best interest. Caesar moved into the royal palace of Alexandria and called a meeting of the fighting siblings to discuss a possible settlement, which he intended to mediate. However, the armies of Ptolemy XIII blocked the return of the king's sister to Alexandria. Cleopatra devised a plan to secretly enter the palace and negotiate a meeting with Caesar, knowing that his diplomatic involvement may aid her in reclaiming the throne. Apollodoros, her servant, was introduced to the 52-year-old Roman after she convinced him to wrap her in a carpet (or, according to other accounts, a bag for storing bedclothes).

A pivotal event in the actual Cleopatra's staging of her own life, the picture of a young Cleopatra falling out of an unfurled carpet has been dramatised in almost every film about her, spanning from silent period features to 1999 T.V. miniseries. "She was clearly using all her talents from the moment she arrived on the world stage before Caesar," says Egyptologist Joann Fletcher, author of a new book, Cleopatra the Great.

Cleopatra, like other ancient Egyptian queens, considered herself to be heavenly. Her family was proclaimed gods or goddesses from the moment of their birth. Cleopatra, who was very self-conscious about her appearance, kept her mystery alive by performing elaborate acts of beauty, drawing parallels between herself and the goddesses Isis and Aphrodite, thus shaping the mythology that continues to honour her. Even though Elizabeth Taylor, Vivien Leigh, and Claudette Colbert's portrayals of Cleopatra in Hollywood films are rife with mistakes, embellishments, and anachronisms, they share a passion for spectacle with the actual queen. A master of disguise and clothing, Cleopatra was, according to Fletcher. "She could reinvent herself to suit the occasion, and I think that's a mark of the consummate politician."

Cleopatra won over Rome's future dictator-for-life with her beggarly appearance as she stepped out of the carpet, clothed in her finest but likely slightly dishevelled. The throne of Egypt was restored to Cleopatra with his assistance. Caesar ordered an armistice, but Ptolemy XIII revolted and perished in the Nile during the subsequent civil war, ensuring Cleopatra's secure reign.

Caesar had already tied the knot when Cleopatra gave him a son, and Egyptian tradition required that she wed Ptolemy XIV, her only surviving sibling. In 44 B.C., Caesar was murdered. Cleopatra had Ptolemy XIV as an ally and had him executed so that her son's succession would not be threatened. She also killed Arsinoe, her sister, who had rebelled to strengthen her hold on the kingdom. Cleopatra and her son's life depended on the brutality typical of Egyptian dynastic politics during her time. After removing all internal challenges, Cleopatra governed Egypt, the wealthiest Mediterranean kingdom and the last to maintain its independence from Rome.

# 6.

# JULIUS CAESAR (ROME)

Julius Caesar, a brilliant statesman and military leader who ruled from 46 to 44 BC, altered the trajectory of Roman history (c. 100 BC - 44 BC).

A new line of emperors and renewed optimism for Rome were gifts he bestowed upon the city during his brief reign.

As a member of an aristocratic family, Julius Caesar had a perilous upbringing in the first century BC. Even with all its might, Rome was still too small to manage. Distrust in the aristocracy was high, and restoring order seemed a distant possibility. Militant tyranny seemed to be the only viable option.

To oppose the aristocracy, Caesar allied. He gained many governmental posts as his career progressed, but not necessarily in an honest fashion. His rise to fame was met with both acclaim and controversy by 63 BC.

Governor of Farther Spain was assigned to him despite his fame. The opportunity to loot the locals at will made this a profitable post. After his return to Rome in 60 BC, he was chosen consul the following year, the republic's highest post.

With his newfound authority, Caesar forged alliances with Pompey and Crassus. Crassus was a multimillionaire, whereas Pompey was a military hero who had endured terrible treatment from the Senate. Even though the two men were competitors, the three men created the formidable "first triumvirate," Caesar successfully bridged the gap.

By distributing public lands to Pompey's troops, Caesar hoped to appease them during his time as consul. He orchestrated a riot and took advantage of the mayhem to pass the proposal, even though it was unpopular. Afterwards, he used his authority to become the governor of Gaul, which included what is now France and Belgium.

Caesar owes much of his fame and wealth to the military wars he led, which he could launch from Gaul.

Using his knowledge of military strategy and the discipline and training of the Roman army, Caesar subjugated the remainder of Gaul, up to the Rhine River, between 58 and 50 BC.

Caesar was tyrannical while fighting foreign foes. After waiting for the rebels' water supply to run out, he beheaded everyone who remained alive while besieging them in what is now the Dordogne region of France.

Now, he was focusing on getting home. There was a lot of tension in his trio. Even while Crassus despised Pompey, his jealousy of Caesar's prosperity grew. Pompey and Caesar became estranged and later found themselves on opposite sides after Crassus died in combat.

Caesar was now very successful, but he faced several adversaries who threatened his position and his life. He reasoned that assuming authority was his one option for self-defence. He invaded Italy in January 49 BC with his army and sparked a civil war.

Caesar became Rome's dictator in 46 BC after several early wins. He spent a year eradicating his last surviving adversaries before returning home. He was kind after his triumph, pardoning all his beaten enemies and even asking a few to serve as his ministers.

But he was still not sure about his future. In the absence of his son, he needed a successor. Adopting Augustus, his great-nephew, was a fast decision for Caesar. He also took rapid action to fortify the empire's northern frontiers and counter its eastern foes.

Domestically, he oversaw reforms to the Roman calendar, municipal governments, veteran resettlement, Senate representation, and citizenship for many non-citizens.

However, his reign would be brief. Frustrated by his autocratic rule, his adversaries banded together with a few of his admirers. The assassination of Caesar took place in the Senate on March 15, 44 BC, often known as the Ides of March.

Even though his reign was uneventful, his triumph in the Civil War transformed a republic governed by senators and consuls into an empire controlled by emperors and their hereditary descendants. Rome entered a new era at that moment.

# 7.

# GEORGE WASHINGTON (USA)

He was born into a planter family in Virginia in 1732 and acquired the education, manners, and character traits expected of a gentleman in the 18th century.

His passions for the military arts and the westward expansion were inseparable. In the summer of 1633, he accompanied Thomas, Lord Fairfax, on a reconnaissance of the Shenandoah. He participated in the first skirmishes of the conflict that would later be known as the French and Indian War after being appointed lieutenant colonel in 1754. The next year, while serving as an assistant to General Edward Braddock, he narrowly avoided harm despite two horses being shot from under him and four bullets ripping his coat.

Washington was a Virginia House of Burgesses member and overseer of the estate around Mount Vernon from 1759 until the Revolutionary War broke out. Martha Dandridge Custis was a widow when he married her, and he continued to lead an active and fulfilling life. Nevertheless, Washington shared his fellow planters' sentiments that the British merchants and rules imposed undue hardship on them. He protested the limitations reasonably but assertively as the dispute with the home nation intensified.

Washington, a delegate from Virginia, was chosen to serve as the Continental Army's commander-in-chief at the May 1775 Second Continental Congress in Philadelphia. He led his poorly equipped army into battle on July 3, 1775, at Cambridge, Massachusetts, and the brutal six-year war began.

He quickly concluded that harassing the British was the most effective tactic. "We ought never to be drawn into a necessity," he told Congress, adding, "We should on all Occasions avoid a general Action or put anything to the Risque." He retreated slowly and then struck unexpectedly in the subsequent fights. At last, in 1781, he succeeded in having Cornwallis capitulated at Yorktown with the help of his French friends.

Washington wished he could retire to Mount Vernon's pastures. However, he quickly realised that the Nation was not working properly under the Articles of Confederation, and he played a key role in the events leading up to the 1787 Constitutional Convention in Philadelphia. The Electoral College overwhelmingly chose Washington as President upon ratifying the new Constitution.

He refrained from trampling on the authority Congress supposedly had under the Constitution to establish national policy. However, the President's involvement in deciding foreign policy became paramount. Even though the French Revolution escalated into a devastating war between England and France, Washington did not blindly follow the advice of his pro-French Secretary of State, Thomas Jefferson or his pro-British Secretary of the Treasury, Alexander Hamilton. Instead, he advocated remaining neutral until American might could be restored.

By the time his first term came to a close, he was disappointed to see the formation of two factions. Feeling elderly and weary of politics, he resigned at the conclusion of his second term. He begged his fellow citizens to put aside their partisanship and regional differences in his farewell address. He cautioned against lasting coalitions in international politics.

Washington's three years in retirement at Mount Vernon were cut short when he succumbed to a throat illness on December 14, 1799. The Nation mourned him for months.

# 8.

# ALEXANDER THE GREAT (MACEDONIA)

Alexander the Great, king of Macedonia from 336 to 323 BCE, conquered the Persian empire, sent Macedonian armies to India, and established the Hellenistic system of territorial kingdoms. He was born in Pella, Macedonia, located northwest of Thessaloníki, Greece, and died in Babylon, near Al-Ḥillah, Iraq. Speculative tales about him began during his lifetime, and he went on to become the hero of a full-scale mythology that was based on nothing more than his historical career.

Philip II was born to Olympias, daughter of King Neoptolemus of Epirus, and Philip II in 356 BCE in Pella in Macedonia. From when he was thirteen years old until he was sixteen, he studied under Aristotle, who sparked an interest in philosophy, medicine, and scientific inquiry. However, he would go on to reject Aristotle's restrictive principle that non-Greeks should be held in servitude. In 340, when Philip attacked Byzantium, Alexander was left in control of Macedonia and vanquished the Thracian Maedi. After two years, he oversaw the left flank in the Battle of Chaeronea, when Philip vanquished the united Greek nations and showed great personal bravery by capturing the Sacred Band of Thebes, a select military unit of 150 couples. Alexander and his mother escaped to Epirus, while Alexander subsequently moved to Illyria after a disagreement during a feast commemorating his father's second marriage, which occurred a year after Philip's divorce from Olympias. Father and son made up a short time later, and Alexander came back, but his succession was in danger.

Nevertheless, Alexander, who had been lauded by the troops, triumphed without resistance in 336 upon Philip's murder. Immediately after becoming certain that the princes of Lyncestis were responsible for Philip's death, he put an end to any potential competitors and the whole opposition group. After reclaiming a faltering Thessaly, he marched south and was named generalissimo for Philip's planned invasion of Asia at a Greek League of Corinth gathering. In the spring of 335, he returned to Macedonia via Delphi, where the Pythian priestess had proclaimed him "invincible." After conquering the Triballi and forcing the Shipka Pass, he crossed the Danube to scatter the Getae. He then turned west, vanquished, and shattered a coalition of Illyrians who had invaded Macedonia. Athenians, encouraged by Demosthenes, decided to aid Thebes after hearing rumours of his death, which sparked a democratic uprising among Theban citizens. Other Greek states supported Thebes. Alexander travelled 240 miles from Pelion in Illyria to Thebes in under 14 days, passing close to modern-day Korçë in Albania. He broke into Theba's city and levelled it to the ground when the inhabitants refused to submit; he spared only the temples and Pindar's mansion, killing 6,000 people and enslaving the rest. Alexander treated Athens leniently because the other Greek nations were intimidated by this harshness. The cities of Corinth, Chalcis, and the Cadmea (Thebes's castle) still had Macedonian garrisons.

# 9.

# QUEEN ELIZABETH II (UK)

Queen Elizabeth II, who passed away on September 8, 2022, at the age of 96, was the queen with the longest tenure in British history. Although she was not initially in direct succession to the throne, she became the heir apparent at age 10 when her father ascended to the monarchy due to the abdication of her uncle, King Edward VIII. The hallmark of her rule was her unwavering commitment to service, which she had shown even before she became queen. During World War II, as an adolescent, she engaged in radio broadcasting to enhance the morale of the British populace. Upon reaching 18, she enlisted in the women's division of the British Army, where she received training in automotive mechanics. During a speech on her 21st birthday, Elizabeth said, "I solemnly affirm to you that my entire existence, regardless of its duration, will be dedicated to serving you and our esteemed imperial family, to which we all belong."

While she refrained from making political declarations during Elizabeth II's global travels, her formal participation at events had the weight of diplomatic comments. She engaged in around 300 public engagements annually. Throughout her reign, she had regular meetings with prime ministers, a total of fifteen, beginning with Winston Churchill and concluding with Liz Truss, a mere two days before her death.

There were also jovial occurrences, such as the queen's tea gathering with Paddington Bear. She started the 2012 Olympics by presenting an intricate film in which she was swiftly transported to a helicopter by Daniel Craig, assuming the role of James Bond. Subsequently, an Elizabeth look-alike, adorned in a parachute, descended into the opening ceremonies.

Queen Elizabeth II maintained her regular appearances and responsibilities until her last year, during which she reduced her commitments solely based on medical recommendations. On her Silver Jubilee in 1977, she contemplated her first commitment to serve. She said, "Although I made that pledge during my youthful and inexperienced years, I have no regrets or reservations about it."

# 10.

# ADOLF HITLER (GERMANY)

Adolf Hitler, the head of Germany's Nazi Party, was a very influential and infamous ruler in the 20th century. Following his service in the German military during World War I, Hitler used economic hardships, widespread dissatisfaction, and internal conflicts within the Weimar Republic to ascend within the hierarchy of the Nazi Party.

Through a sequence of merciless and aggressive acts, such as the Reichstag Fire or the Night of Long Knives, Hitler successfully seized complete control over Germany by 1933. The invasion of Poland by Germany in 1939 precipitated the commencement of World War II. By the end of 1941, Nazi troops had used "blitzkrieg" military strategies to seize control of a significant portion of Europe. Hitler's extreme hatred for Jews and his relentless quest for Aryan dominance led to the systematic killing of about 6 million Jews, as well as other victims of the Holocaust. Hitler took his own life in a Berlin bunker in April 1945 as the war started to go against him.

Adolf Hitler was born on April 20, 1889, in Braunau am Inn, a tiny village in Austria located on the border between Austria and Germany.

Following his father's retirement as a state customs agent, Adolf spent most of his early years in Linz, the principal city of Upper Austria.

Disinclined to pursue a career as a government servant like his father, he had difficulties in secondary school and ultimately withdrew. Alois passed away in 1903, and Adolf endeavoured to fulfil his aspiration of becoming an artist despite rejection from Vienna's Academy of Fine Arts.

Following the death of his mother, Klara, in 1908, Hitler relocated to Vienna. He earned a livelihood there by creating paintings of landscapes and landmarks, which he then sold. Hitler, who was lonely, secluded, and had a strong passion for reading, became intrigued by politics while living in Vienna. It was at this time that he formulated many of the concepts that would later influence Nazi ideology.

Hitler and Eva Braun were married in the Berlin bunker on the night of April 28-29, precisely at midnight. Following the dictation of his political testament, Hitler committed himself in his suite on April 30 while Braun ingested poison. Hitler's directives incinerated their remains.

On May 7, 1945, Germany surrendered without any conditions to Soviet soldiers who were occupying Berlin, thereby ending the war in Europe.

Ultimately, Hitler's envisioned "Thousand-Year Reich" lasted for more than 12 years but inflicted immeasurable ruin and misery over that period, permanently altering the course of Germany, Europe, and the globe.

# 11.

# ABRAHAM LINCOLN (USA)

Abraham Lincoln was born on February 12, 1809, in a small log cabin in Hardin County, Kentucky. His familial background was humble; his parents, hailing from Virginia, were neither affluent nor renowned. During his childhood, Abraham Lincoln experienced his mother's loss and his father's departure to Indiana. Abraham exerted significant effort in doing tasks such as splitting wood and engaging in physical labour. However, he also had a strong desire for information and exerted significant effort to achieve excellence in his academic pursuits.

Consequently, he embarked on a journey of self-education to acquire the skills and knowledge necessary to practise law. For eight years, he dedicated himself to serving on the Illinois court circuit, displaying his ambition, determination, and ability to work diligently, which were apparent to everyone in his vicinity. Lincoln earned high respect in the legal field and was given the moniker 'Honest Abe'. He often urged neighbours to resolve their issues via mediation instead of formal judicial proceedings. Additionally, Lincoln had a keen sense of humour and was self-deprecating regarding his appearance.

Colleagues and friends observed that Lincoln can alleviate stressful and contentious circumstances by using humour and maintaining an optimistic perspective on human nature. He had a penchant for using comedy and parables to convey a profound message.

Lincoln overcame obstacles throughout their romance despite his shyness with women and eventually married Mary Todd in 1842. Mary Todd had a considerable alignment with her husband's political ideology. However, their temperaments diverged, with Mary displaying a greater susceptibility to fluctuations in her emotional state. Lincoln was dedicated to his four children. Despite the fact that three individuals perished before reaching adulthood, this unfortunate circumstance brought immense sorrow to both parents.

Abraham, being a lawyer, honed his ability to think quickly and deliver persuasive speeches. His inclination in public affairs motivated him to run for a political position. In 1847, he was elected as a member of the House of Representatives representing Illinois and held the position from 1847 to 1849. While serving in Congress, Lincoln voiced his disapproval of President Polk's management of the American-Mexican War. He said that Polk used patriotism and military triumph to justify the unlawful act of annexing Mexican land. Nevertheless, Lincoln's position was politically unfavourable, resulting in his failure to secure re-election.

Braham Lincoln, as depicted following the seeming conclusion of his political tenure, resumed his profession as a lawyer in Illinois. Nevertheless, in the 1850s, the topic of slavery resurfaced as a significant and polarising matter on a national scale. Lincoln detested slavery and, from a political standpoint, aimed to prohibit its expansion and finally eliminate it.

He delivered impactful lectures and used the Declaration of Independence as evidence to demonstrate the Founding Fathers' intention to halt the expansion of slavery. Specifically, Lincoln used an innovative rationale that despite the considerable distance society had yet to traverse to achieve equality, America should strive towards the elevated principle articulated in the Declaration of Independence.

# 12.

# MAO ZEDONG (CHINA)

The unplanned meeting between "Chairman Mao Tse-tung and Richard Nixon" lasted for just over an hour, was the pinnacle of the president's diplomatic visit to China in February 1972. Both Nixon and his national security advisor Henry Kissinger were deeply impressed by the 78-year-old chairman, who, as Kissinger later recounted in his memoirs, "commanded the room" with a palpable determination to succeed.

Mao Tse-tung, as the paramount leader and chief strategist of the Chinese Communist Party (CCP), is primarily linked to both the achievements and setbacks of the Communist Revolution. Mao, one of the first members of the Chinese Communist Party (CCP) in 1921, significantly impacted his political ideology due to his active participation in the peasant struggle in Hunan. Contrary to the conventional Marxist leaders of the Chinese Communist Party (CCP) who aimed to mobilise the urban proletariat, Mao firmly believed that the Communist revolution in China could only triumph by actively engaging the rural peasants, who constituted eighty percent of the population.

In 1935 Mao led Communist soldiers 6000 miles on the "Long March" across China in retreat from Chiang Kai-shek's Nationalist forces. Upon arriving in Yan'an province, he developed a rural stronghold and cultivated a party that was devoted to him personally. Utilising this foundation, Mao successfully led Communist troops to triumph over the Nationalists during the civil war from 1946 to 1949. Mao founded the People's Republic of China on October 1, 1949. As the Party and the State Chairman, his position had the same authority as that of a president, while Chou En-lai acted as his prime minister.

During Mao's rule, China saw significant societal changes, particularly the emancipation of the peasants from long-standing control by landlords, and the freedom of Chinese women via the revision of restrictive marriage legislation. However, in the late 1950s and 1960s, Mao carried out calamitous economic and social initiatives, resulting in significant human suffering.

Between 1958 and 1962, Mao's "Great Leap Forward" initiative, which aimed to collectivise agriculture and accelerate industrial development, resulted in severe economic devastation in China. Tragically, approximately thirty million Chinese people perished due to starvation during this period. In 1966, Mao initiated a "Great Proletarian Cultural Revolution," which aimed to indoctrinate a fresh cohort of revolutionaries and eliminate Mao's political adversaries inside the CCP. With the support of the military, numerous students organised themselves into Red Guard units. They embarked on a mission to eliminate institutions and individuals in China who were considered not revolutionary enough. Like the Great Leap Forward, the Cultural Revolution resulted in extensive economic turmoil. The event resulted in the demise of over two million individuals, including numerous scholars, intellectuals, and artists.

At the time of Nixon's visit in 1972, China started recovering from the most severe period of the Cultural Revolution. However, many of its policies and institutions were not completely abandoned until Mao died in 1976.

Throughout the Cultural Revolution, Mao attained a position of almost divine reverence. His likeness, prominently displayed on banners and badges, became omnipresent throughout China, and his aphorisms, accurately replicated in the "Little Red Book," were often cited. In 1981, the Chinese Communist Party (CCP) embraced an official party stance that condemned Mao for the extreme actions of the Cultural Revolution, while commending the initial period of his leadership. During the 1980s, there was a surge in literary and historical curiosity about China, particularly focusing on the intimate aspects of Mao's life. In recent years, Mao has gained prominence as a prominent figure in Chinese pop music and art, with some of it being satirical. This reflects the ongoing struggle of the nation to fully comprehend and deal with Mao's enduring impact.

# 13.

# GENGHIS KHAN (MONGOL EMPIRE)

Genghis Khan was a legendary Mongolian warrior-ruler who united many tribes into a single nation and expanded his empire to the Adriatic Sea. He was born in 1162 near Lake Baikal in Mongolia and died on August 18, 1227.

Genghis Khan, a brilliant commander and warrior, rose from humble origins to unite the nomadic Mongolian tribes under a strict military dictatorship he and his family established. He shifted his focus to the people who had settled outside his nomadic kingdom and launched a string of conquest and plunder campaigns that would eventually establish the great Mongol Empire, stretching its armies as far as the Adriatic Sea and the Pacific coast of China, respectively.

Nearly all of what is known about Genghis Khan's life comes from non-Mongol sources, except the saga-like Secret History of the Mongols (1240?). Even authors who served the Mongols have focused on the immense devastation caused by their conquests. When reminded of these, one Arab scholar spoke out in open dismay. Matthew Paris, a historian from the 13th century who relied on second-hand accounts and was outside the Mongols' sphere of influence, characterized them as a "detestable nation of Satan that poured out like devils from Tartarus so that they are rightly called Tartars." Although his story captures the fear that the Mongols inspired, it is clear that he was attempting a pun using the classical term Tartarus (Hell) and the old tribal name Tatar, which was carried by some of the nomads. Genghis Khan shares his people's reputation as the Mongol country's creator, organizer of the Mongol armies, and mastermind behind their conquests, even though his generals sometimes acted without direct supervision. However, portraying the Mongol invasions as random raids by nomadic nomads is inaccurate. Furthermore, contrary to popular belief, these campaigns were not triggered by the gradual drying up of Inner Asia, which forced the nomads to seek fresh pastures.

Furthermore, the Mongol invasions were not an isolated incident. Although he was one among many, Genghis Khan did not emerge from the Steppe to terrify the settled edge of Eurasia as a nomadic invader. His campaigns were more extensive, fruitful, and long-lasting than his rivals. They impacted a larger portion of the Eurasian continent and a wide range of communities, but they were most devastating to nomadic peoples who kept written records of past events.

Despite their fundamentally different ways of existence, two mutually antagonistic civilizations maintained continual communication and relied on one other. The nomads yearned for the comforts and necessities of the South, but they also required some of its core goods. Trading, taxing, passing caravans, or armed attacks might all lead to their acquisition. Chinese settlers had a smaller need for steppe goods, but they couldn't ignore the nomadic nomads and were always worried about fending off their advances. When a dynasty is powerful enough, as the Manchu in the 17th century, it may use its military might to control all of Inner Asia directly. On other occasions, the Chinese would need to manipulate the barbarians by pitting one group against another, shifting allegiances and transferring support to keep any tribe from becoming too powerful.

In parallel with the rise and fall of Chinese dynasties, the steppe peoples went through periods of unity and disintegration. Nomadic tribes under a strong leader may, at their strongest, conquer neighbouring tribes and, in a weak China, expand their influence beyond the steppe. Finally, a new enemy emerged due to this expansion of nomadic power into the southern, more settled society. The nomads were engulfed by the Chinese they had conquered, and they lost their customary advantage—that lightning-fast mobility that needed little in the way of food and supplies. The nomads' way of existence would be characterized by disorder and minor disputes among transient chieftains, and the cycle would eventually repeat itself with a mighty China reemerging. Genghis Khan's life must be assessed against this backdrop of political tensions and contradictions, and the Mongol conquests' history does a superb job of illustrating this aspect. The results of his wars were not some unexplained natural or divine disaster but rather the product of a series of events orchestrated by a brilliant, ambitious, and determined soldier. At a time when China and other established governments were declining for various reasons, he took advantage of the fact that his tribal world was prepared for union.

# 14.

# MARGARET THATCHER (UK)

Primrose was born from 1979 to 1990, and the first woman in Europe, Margaret Thatcher, was born on October 13, 1925, in Grantham, Lincolnshire, England, and died on April 8, 2013, in London. She was a member of the Conservative Party in Britain. She expedited the transition of the British economy from statism to liberalism. Through her charisma, as much as her accomplishments, she became the most famous British political figure since Winston Churchill. She was the only prime minister of the twentieth century to win three consecutive terms and the longest-serving prime minister until her resignation. Prime Minister Liz Truss looked up to her.

Early on in Thatcher's life, she had ambitions of becoming a politician; her parents were Alfred Roberts, a grocer and local alderman (who would later become mayor of Grantham), and Beatrice Ethel Stephenson. At Oxford, she studied chemistry thanks to her brilliant mind, but she was already involved in politics, becoming one of the first female presidents of the Oxford University Conservative

Association. She was a research chemist for four years after finishing college in 1947, during which time she also studied for legal exams in her leisure time. She began her career as a barrister in 1954, focusing on tax law. Denis Thatcher, a rich businessman who married her in 1951 and encouraged her political ambitions, was born in 1915 and died in 2003. It was in 1953 that the couple welcomed a set of twins—a boy and a girl.

Despite a 50% increase in the local Conservative vote, Thatcher's 1950 attempt for Parliament was unsuccessful. She became a member of Parliament in 1959 after being elected to the Conservatives' "safe" northern London constituency of Finchley. She worked her way up the ranks of the Conservative Party, eventually becoming secretary of state for education and science in Edward Heath's administration (1970–1974), chief spokesperson for the opposition on education (1969–1970), and "parliamentary secretary in the Ministry of Pensions and National Insurance" (1961–1964). The elimination of a programme that offered free milk to schoolchildren caused a storm of controversy. It led Thatcher's opponents in the Labour Party to taunt her, calling her "Thatcher the milk snatcher." At the time, she was a member of the Heath cabinet (the only woman to hold a cabinet portfolio in a Conservative government). Although she oversaw undermining comprehensive schools as prime minister, she was the first education minister in history to establish more of them than any other. The Labour Party had established comprehensive schools in the 1960s to ensure that students from working-class backgrounds may have access to a high academic education. Even though she was low in the party hierarchy, Thatcher was the only minister willing to challenge Heath for the party leadership when he lost two consecutive elections in 1974. She started a 15-year rise that would alter Britain's face when, in February 1975, she was elected leader with the support of the conservative right wing.

# 15.

# NAPOLEON BONAPARTE (FRANCE)

The two-time French emperor Napoleon Bonaparte (August 15, 1769–May 5, 1821) was legendary in European politics and military history. His charisma and achievements commanded attention for ten years.

His deeds shaped the trajectory of European history for more than a century—and, some contend, even until the present day—in matters of law, economics, politics, technology, culture, and society at large.

Napoleon was born to Carlo Buonaparte and Marie-Letizia in Ajaccio, Corsica, on August 15, 1769. Carlo was a political opportunist and a lawyer. Though impoverished compared to the great French aristocracies, Napoleon's relatives from the affluent Buonaparte family were originally from Corsica.

In 1779, Napoleon enrolled in the Brienne Military Academy. He enrolled at the École Royale Militaire in Paris in 1784 and became a second lieutenant in the artillery the following year after graduating. The impending emperor's father's death in 1785 served as a spur to finish the course in one year, even though it normally takes three.

A combination of Napoleon's fierce letter writing, rule-bending, the French Revolution (which sparked the French Revolutionary Wars), and good fortune allowed him to spend a significant portion of the following eight years in Corsica, even though he was assigned to the French mainland. He was heavily involved in military and political affairs there, first lending his support to the Corsican rebel Pasquale Paoli, who had previously been Carlo Buonaparte's sponsor.

The Buonaparte family likewise rose through the ranks of the French military. However, Napoleon's animosity against Paoli led to the 1793 outbreak of civil war, and the Buonaparte family eventually settled in France, changing their surname to Bonaparte.

In a republic where the Revolution had wiped out the officer class, favouritism allowed for rapid advancement; nonetheless, Napoleon's fortunes fluctuated with each new group of supporters. Though he had become a favourite of Augustin Robespierre and a hero to the people of Toulon by December 1793, the revolutionary wheel soon turned, and Napoleon was imprisoned for treason. The support of Vicomte Paul de Barras, who would later become one of France's three "Directors," and his extraordinary political pliability rescued him.

In 1795, Napoleon again became a hero when he defended the government against furious counter-revolutionary elements. As a result, Baras promoted Napoleon to a high military post, giving him access to France's political spine. In 1796, Napoleon wed Josephine de Beauharnais, and soon after, he became one of the most revered military leaders in the nation, mostly because he never kept his views to himself.

# 16.

# VLADIMIR LENIN (RUSSIA)

Lenin was a prominent figure in 20th-century politics and revolutionary thought. He was instrumental in the 1917 Bolshevik coup d'état in Russia and served as the country's first leader.

In the city of Simbirsk on the Volga River, Vladimir Ilich Ulyanov came into this world on April 22, 1870, into a family that valued education. He was a straight-A student who went on to become a lawyer. Both the radical ideas he encountered at university, and the killing of his revolutionary brother profoundly impacted his worldview.

Lenin earned his law degree in 1891 while studying as an external student after being expelled from university due to his radical views. He became a professional revolutionary after relocating to St. Petersburg. He was imprisoned and sent to Siberia, where he wed Nadezhda Krupskaya, much like many of his contemporaries. A prominent figure in the worldwide revolutionary movement and the leader of the 'Bolshevik' faction of the Russian Social Democratic Worker's Party,

Lenin—a pseudonym he adopted in 1901—spent the majority of the next fifteen years in Western Europe after his exile in Siberia.

After being worn down by WWI, Russia was ready for a change in 1917. Lenin went back to Russia and began fighting against the interim government that had deposed the tsarist rule, with the help of the Germans, who wanted him to derail the Russian war effort. The October Revolution, which he finally led, was really a coup d'état, but it gained momentum under his leadership. The subsequent civil war lasted for almost three years. After their triumph, the Bolsheviks took full power in Russia. Throughout this time of upheaval, Lenin showed a sick callousness for the plight of his compatriots and ruthlessly quelled any resistance.

Lenin was a realist despite his vicious nature. His New Economic Policy, which allowed for some private industry again after his attempts to convert the Russian economy to a socialist model failed, persisted for a number of years after he passed away. Despite suffering serious injuries, Lenin managed to evade an assassination attempt in 1918. His health, in the long run, took a hit, and he had a stroke in 1922, which he never got over completely. Aware of the regime's bureaucratization and his future successor Joseph Stalin's growing influence, he voiced concerns in his latter years. Lenin passed away on January 24, 1924. His body was laid to rest in a mausoleum on Red Square in Moscow after being embalmed.

# 17.

# MARTIN LUTHER KING JR. (USA)

Born on January 15, 1929, in Atlanta, Georgia, United States, and killed on April 4, 1968, in Memphis, Tennessee, Martin Luther King, Jr. was a Baptist preacher and social activist who spearheaded the American civil rights movement from the mid-1950s until his murder in 1968. The success of the effort to remove legal segregation of African Americans in the South and other regions of the US was greatly influenced by his leadership. King became a household name after taking the helm of the Southern Christian Leadership Conference, which advocated for civil rights via nonviolent means, including the 1963 March on Washington. The Nobel Peace Prize was bestowed upon him in 1964.

Because his father and maternal grandparents were Baptist ministers, King grew up in a comfortable middle-class household deeply rooted in the history of Black ministry in the South. King's parents had advanced degrees; the father had replaced the father-in-law as pastor of Atlanta's esteemed Ebenezer Baptist Church. Before the civil rights struggle, the family's house on Auburn Avenue—also called "Sweet Auburn"—was a thriving "Black Wall Street" where many of the country's most prominent Black churches and businesses were located. Martin had a supportive extended family and a good education as a child.

Nevertheless, King still encountered the prevalent stereotypes in the South despite his comfortable background. When King was about six years old, a white playmate of his announced that King's parents would no longer let him play with King due to the children's segregated schooling. This incident stayed with him forever. His maternal grandmother was King's rock in his formative years; her untimely death in 1941 left him emotionally fragile. The 12-year-old King went to a second-story window in an attempt at suicide after learning of her deadly heart attack during a parade he had attended without his parents' consent.

A unique wartime programme admitted bright high school pupils like King to Atlanta's Morehouse College in 1944 when he was fifteen years old. The goal was to increase enrollment. Tobacco farming in Connecticut was King's first real exposure to racial relations outside the divided South and his first long stay away from home before starting college. The harmonious racial mixing in the North startled him. "Negroes and whites go [to] the same church," he wrote in a long letter to his parents. "It never occurred to me that someone of my ethnicity could find food anywhere." During his time in the North that summer, King's animosity against racial segregation only intensified.

During his time at Morehouse, King had a strong interest in medicine and law. However, in his last year, he followed his father's advice and joined the ministry. Benjamin Mays, president of Morehouse College and a social gospel crusader whose father King had been profoundly influenced by Mays's eloquent speeches and progressive beliefs, served as King's mentor when the young King was a student there. Mays, who was devoted to the fight against racial inequality, accused African Americans of being complacent in the face of oppression. In an effort to spur social action, he criticised the Black church for focusing on the afterlife rather than the present moment. The adolescent King did not miss this call to service. In 1948, he earned his degree from Morehouse.

# 18.

# JOSEPH STALIN (USSR)

Joseph Stalin, who was born on December 18 (or December 6, Old Style) in Gori, Georgia, Russian Empire and died on March 5, 1953, in Moscow, Russia, U.S.S.R., was a Stalinist who ruled the Soviet Union dictatorially for 25 years, from 1922 to 1953 and turned it into a global superpower.

Joseph Stalin, ruler of the Soviet Union, perhaps had more political clout in the quarter of a century leading up to his death than anybody else in history. Stalin expanded Soviet power to cover a belt of eastern European republics, industrialised the Union of Soviet Socialist Republics, forcefully collectivised its agriculture, strengthened its position by intense police brutality, and helped defeat Germany in 1941–1945. He was the mastermind behind Soviet authoritarianism and an incredibly brutal organiser; he took the country into the nuclear era while destroying personal freedoms and failing to help people flourish.

A Soviet-propagated "legend" inflated Stalin's heroics as a Bolshevik boy conspirator and devoted disciple of Lenin, the Soviet Union's founder, and hid the truth about Stalin's life for a long time. Stalin was once publicly referred to as "Our Father" by a metropolitan of the Russian Orthodox Church; during his heyday, he was praised as a "shining sun," "the staff of life," a "great teacher and friend" (particularly among the populations he brutally oppressed), and a universal genius. In private, the dictator likely viewed his obsessive cult with scepticism, but in public, he became well-known for his busts, monuments, and icons, which attracted a devoted following.

Rumour has it that Stalin's paternal line is Ossetian, albeit he was of Georgian descent, not Russian. In the Georgian town of Gori, a colony of imperial Russia at the time, he was born to a poor cobbler. The father brutally thrashed his kid when he was inebriated. Joseph attended the church school in Gori (1888–1894) and studied Russian, which he always spoke using a guttural Georgian accent, even though he spoke solely Georgian at home. According to the "legend" (his mother's version of events), he was expelled in 1899 for revolutionary activity. However, he secretly read Karl Marx, the chief theoretician of international Communism, and other forbidden texts while enrolled at the Tiflis Theological Seminary. Joseph Dzhugashvili was more gangsta than ecclesiastical, which disappointed his mother, a religious washerwoman who had hoped her son would follow in her priestly footsteps. His swarthy face had scars from smallpox received as an infant, and he was short and stocky with black hair and ferocious eyes. One of his arms was longer than the other. In keeping with the Caucasian blood-feud tradition, he was tenacious in planning long-term vengeance against those who wronged him; he was physically powerful and blessed with extraordinary determination, but he learned early on to hide his actual sentiments and wait it out.

There is no record of Dzhugashvili ever having done physical work; the only paid occupation he is known as having outside of politics was a short stint as a clerk in the Tiflis Observatory in December 1899. In 1900, he became a member of the political underground and incited strikes and protests in the major Caucasian industrial cities. However, his fellow conspirators were enraged by his enthusiasm in leading naive workers into violent confrontations with the authorities. Dzhugashvili became a follower of Lenin and a more militant Bolshevik group member when the Russian Empire's Social Democrats (Marxist revolutionaries) divided into two rival groups in 1903. Dzhugashvili was imprisoned and exiled many times for revolutionary action between April 1902 and March 1913. Unsubstantiated rumours have it that Dzhugashvili was once an imperial political police agent provocateur, according to the leniency of his sentences or the ease with which the youthful conspirator managed his many escapes.

# 19.

# JOAN OF ARC (FRANCE)

Saint Joan of Arc, also known as Jeanne d'Arc, was born in 1412 CE in Domrémy, Bar, France. She died on May 30, 1431, at Rouen. She was canonised on May 16, 1920, and her feast day is celebrated on May 30. Joan of Arc is recognised as a French military heroine. From a young age, she was a peasant girl who firmly thought that she could hear the voices of Saints Michael, Catherine, or Margaret. At around the age of 16, she started hearing voices that encouraged her to assist the dauphin of France and protect the country from the English invasion during the Hundred Years' War. Clad in masculine attire, she paid a visit to the dauphin and successfully persuaded him, his advisors, and the ecclesiastical authorities to lend their backing to her cause. Through her compelling determination, she mobilised the French forces and successfully lifted the English blockade of Orléans in 1429. She swiftly triumphed against the English once more at Patay. Charles VII was crowned as king at Reims, with Joan by his side. Despite her attempt to conquer Paris, she was unable to succeed. In 1430, she was taken prisoner by the Burgundians before being sold to the English. After being abandoned by Charles, she was handed over to the ecclesiastical court at Rouen, which was under the hands of French clerics who were supportive of the English. She was then subjected to a trial for witchcraft and heresy in 1431. She vigorously defended herself but ultimately retracted her statement and was subsequently condemned to life imprisonment. Upon reiterating her claim of divine inspiration, she was sent to execution by burning at the stake.

Roman Catholicism is the most populous Christian denomination, boasting a membership of over one billion individuals. The Roman Catholic Church has had a significant influence on the development of Western culture and has played a pivotal role in disseminating Christianity throughout various regions globally. The organisation considers itself the only rightful successor of Jesus' ministry, based on an uninterrupted lineage of leaders starting with St. Peter the Apostle and extending to the current day. According to this belief, the pope has the ability to accurately interpret heavenly revelation without error. The structure of the church organisation is characterised by a tight hierarchy. The pope selects and leads the cardinals, whose ranks saw a significant increase in the latter part of the 20th century, reaching a total of 182 during the papacy of John Paul II (1978-2005). Every one of the church's 500 archbishops serves as the leader of an archdiocese. These are further categorised into around 1,800 dioceses, with each diocese being led by a bishop. Dioceses consist of parishes, each of which is attended to by a church priest. The priesthood is only open to males, whereas women who want to join religious orders may pursue the path of becoming nuns. Nuns are organised into orders and reside in convents. The fundamental mode of religious reverence is the mass, a ritual that commemorates the sacrament of the Eucharist. Roman Catholicism and Protestantism diverge theologically in their perspectives on the origins of divine revelation and the means through which grace is transmitted. Eastern Orthodoxy maintains that both scripture and church tradition are sources of divine revelation for Christian doctrine and church governance. The Catholic Church establishes the number of sacraments as seven, which include baptism, reconciliation (previously known as penance), the Eucharist, marriage, ordination, confirmation, and anointing of the sick. In addition to these sacraments, the Catholic Church also practises various devotions, mostly centred upon eucharistic rites and devotion to the saints. The

Second Vatican Council (1962–65) advocated for the involvement of laypeople in the church, sanctioned the use of the native language in the mass, and endeavoured to enhance interfaith ties. Pope John Paul II vigorously sought to improve ties with other religions, particularly Judaism and maintained widespread popularity despite several problems. Despite encountering several obstacles, the church maintained its position as one of the greatest and most influential religious organisations globally as it entered its third millennium.

# 20.

# OTTO VON BISMARCK (GERMANY)

Bismarck played a pivotal role in converting a group of little German nations into the German empire, assuming the position of its first chancellor.

Otto Eduard Leopold von Bismarck was born on April 1,1 April, 1815 in Schönhausen, located northwest of Berlin. He was born into a family belonging to the aristocracy. He enrolled at a renowned Berlin institution and pursued his education at the University of Göttingen. Subsequently, he joined the Prussian civil service but found his position monotonous and decided to retire in 1838. Over a period of over ten years, he assisted his father in overseeing the family properties.

In 1847, Bismarck entered matrimony with Johanna von Puttkamer, whose presence bestowed a sense of steadiness and constancy. During that year, he experienced substantial transformations in his life. He also adopted the Christian denomination of Lutheranism and started his political journey in the Prussian assembly, where he earned recognition as an extremely conservative supporter of the monarchy.

King Frederick Wilhelm IV designated Bismarck as the Prussian envoy to the German Confederation in 1851. Subsequently, he assumed the role of ambassador to both Russia and France. Upon his return to Prussia in 1862, he was designated as prime minister by the newly crowned monarch, Wilhelm I.

Bismarck was resolute in consolidating the German nations into a unified empire, with Prussia as its central component. With the assistance of Austria, Alexander used the augmented Prussian military force to seize control of the Schleswig and Holstein territories from Denmark. Subsequently, he intensified a dispute with Austria and its German allies on the governance of these regions, leading to a conflict in which Prussia emerged as the triumphant party. Subsequently, Prussia proceeded to incorporate further land inside Germany.

Incapable of convincing the southern German states to join his North German Confederation, he deliberately instigated conflicts with France to consolidate the German nations. The triumph of Germany in the Franco-Prussian War resulted in the southern German states being persuaded to unite with a German empire in 1871. Wilhelm I of Prussia ascended to the position of emperor.

In his role as the 'chancellor' of the newly formed Germany, Bismarck focused on constructing a robust state with a cohesive national character. One of his objectives was to undermine the Catholic Church, as he saw it to possess excessive influence, especially in southern Germany. In addition, he attempted to impede the proliferation of socialism by implementing measures such as introducing health insurance or pensions.

Throughout his time abroad, Bismarck aimed to establish the German empire as the dominant force in Europe. In 1879, he forged a diplomatic partnership with Austria-Hungary to counterbalance France and Russia's influence. Italy subsequently became a member of the alliance. In order to prevent Britain from becoming estranged, Bismarck orchestrated the two Mediterranean Agreements of 1887, which were intended to maintain the existing state of affairs in response to a potential Russian danger.

In 1890, Bismarck tendered his resignation due to a divergence of opinions with the newly ascended monarch, Wilhelm II. He retired to his property close to Hamburg and passed away there on 30 July 1898.

# 21.

# THEODORE ROOSEVELT (USA)

Roosevelt served as the 26th president of the United States, exhibiting robust leadership and significantly broadening American engagement in international matters.

Theodore Roosevelt was born in New York on October 27, 1858, as the offspring of an affluent entrepreneur. In 1876, he enrolled at Harvard University and attended Columbia Law School. In 1881, he departed from his studies to campaign for a New York State Assembly position. He was first elected as a member of the Republican party and then re-elected twice, becoming leadership of the Republican party. In 1884, he worked as a cattle rancher in the Dakota Territory for two years. Subsequently, he transitioned into a profession as a writer, producing a comprehensive four-volume account of America's westward expansion, published between 1889 and 1896.

Benjamin Harrison, the Republican President in 1889, designated him as a US Civil Service Commission member. In 1895, Roosevelt assumed the presidency of the New York City police board. In the following year, he was designated as the assistant secretary of the navy by Republican President William McKinley. Roosevelt ardently advocated for expanding US naval capabilities as a strategic approach to bolstering America's global influence. Throughout the Spanish-American War, Roosevelt actively served as a lieutenant colonel in the Rough Rider Regiment.

Roosevelt was elected governor of New York in 1898 and served as vice president under McKinley in 1900. Roosevelt became President in September 1901 after the assassination of McKinley. In 1904, he was elected independently and without any external influence. His administration was distinguished by implementing anti-monopolistic measures aimed at curbing the influence of major enterprises. Furthermore, he founded the first national park in the United States, located in Florida, in 1903 and the initial national monument in Wyoming in 1906.

Roosevelt advocated for a diplomatic approach to international relations, emphasising the need to use force as a deterrent. He believed the United States' security would be strengthened when other countries knew the US would safeguard its interests by employing the prospect of armed conflict. The corollary he proposed to the Monroe Doctrine effectively prohibited the development of foreign military installations in the Caribbean region and asserted the exclusive authority of the United States to intervene in Latin American affairs. Roosevelt also promoted the construction of the Panama Canal. He received the Nobel Peace Prize in 1906 for his contribution to resolving the Russo-Japanese conflict.

Roosevelt concluded his tenure as President in 1908. In the 1912 presidential election, he competed against his successor, William Taft, whose policies he strongly opposed. The Republican support was divided by his candidature, which ultimately resulted in the election of Democrat Woodrow Wilson as President. Roosevelt passed away on January 6, 1919. The moniker 'Teddy' has endured and become associated with the teddy bear.

# 22.

# SIMON BOLIVAR (VENEZUELA)

Simón Bolívar, born on July 24, 1783, in Caracas, Venezuela (then part of New Granada, now Venezuela), and died on December 17, 1830, in Santa Marta, Colombia, was a Venezuelan soldier and politician. He was pivotal in leading the revolutions against Spanish control in the Viceroyalty of New Granada. He served as the ruler of Gran Colombia from 1819 to 1830 and held the position of dictator in Peru from 1823 to 1826.

Bolívar, born into affluence and social standing, was the offspring of a Venezuelan aristocracy of Spanish ancestry. At the age of three, the boy's father passed away, and six years later, his mother also died. Subsequently, his uncle managed his fortune and arranged for tutors to educate him. One of those teachers, Simón Rodríguez, had a profound and enduring impact on him. Rodríguez, who followed the teachings of Jean-Jacques Rousseau, exposed Bolívar to the ideas of 18th-century liberalism.

Bolívar was sent to Europe at the age of 16 in order to conclude his schooling. He resided in Spain for three years, and in 1801, he entered into matrimony with the offspring of a Spanish aristocrat. Subsequently, he accompanied his spouse back to Caracas. The youthful bride succumbed to yellow fever within a year after their nuptials. Bolívar attributed his decision to pursue a political career at an early age to the untimely death of the woman he deeply mourned.

In 1804, at the height of Napoleon I's success, Bolívar travelled back to Europe. While in Paris, he immersed himself in the works of prominent European rationalist philosophers, including John Locke, Thomas Hobbes, Georges-Louis Leclerc, Count de Buffon, Jean le Rond d'Alembert, and Claude-Adrien Helvétius. Additionally, he studied the writings of Voltaire, Montesquieu, and Rousseau under the guidance of his friend and tutor Rodríguez. The latter two had the most profound impact on his political activity, while Voltaire imbued his philosophy of life. While in Paris, Bolívar encountered the German scientist Alexander von Humboldt, who had just completed his expedition across Hispanic America. Von Humboldt expressed his belief to Bolívar that the Spanish colonies were ready to achieve independence. The concept firmly established itself in Bolívar's mind, and on a visit to Rome with Rodríguez, when they were standing on the elevated grounds of Monte Sacro, he made a solemn promise to free his homeland.

Another event that enhanced his mind during that period was seeing the remarkable spectacle that concluded with Napoleon's coronation in 1804 as the emperor of France. Bolívar's response to the coronation oscillated between appreciation for the achievements of an individual and disgust at Napoleon's betrayal of the principles of the French Revolution. Bolívar's temperament had a lasting inclination towards seeking glory, and Napoleon likely influenced this inclination. However, Bolívar took notice of the example of Napoleon as a warning. In his final years, he consistently maintained that the designation of "liberator" had more significance than any other title, and he adamantly refused to trade it for the positions of king or emperor. In 1807, he returned to Venezuela via the United States, where he visited the towns in the eastern region.

# 23.

# ELIZABETH I (UK)

Elizabeth I was born on September 7, 1533, in Greenwich, near London, England. She passed away on March 24, 1603, in Richmond, Surrey. Elizabeth I reigned as the queen of England from 1558 to 1603. Her reign, known as the Elizabethan Age, was a time when England emerged as a prominent European force in politics, trade, and the arts.

Despite facing significant internal conflicts, Elizabeth's astuteness, bravery, and grandiose self-presentation evoked fervent displays of allegiance and contributed to the unification of the country in the face of external adversaries. The admiration given to Mary, both during her life and in the following centuries, was not entirely a spontaneous outpouring. The outcome was the product of a well-planned and skillfully carried out campaign in which the queen portrayed herself as the dazzling embodiment of the nation's future. This political symbolism, which is often seen in monarchs, had a greater significance than normal since the queen was not only a symbolic leader. Although she did not possess the whole authority that Renaissance monarchs aspired to, she firmly maintained her capacity to make crucial choices and establish the fundamental policies of both the state and the church. The latter portion of the 16th century in England is rightfully referred to as the Elizabethan Age. It is uncommon to find an entire era that has been so uniquely characterised by the personal influence of one individual.

Following her father's death in 1547 and the ascension of her weak 10-year-old brother Edward to the kingdom, Elizabeth's life became fraught with danger. Shortly after, Catherine Parr, the former queen dowager, promptly wed Thomas Seymour, the esteemed lord high admiral. Seymour, who was attractive, ambitious, and dissatisfied, started to plot against his influential elder brother, Edward Seymour, who was the defender of the kingdom during Edward VI's period as a juvenile. In January 1549, after the death of Catherine Parr, Thomas Seymour was apprehended on charges of treason and alleged conspiracy to wed Elizabeth with the intention of assuming control over the country. Through many interrogations, Elizabeth and her servants consistently accused Seymour of engaging in flirty and excessively familiar behaviour towards the young princess, even while his wife was still alive. Elizabeth displayed remarkable composure and caution while being subjected to degrading and intense interrogation, putting herself at risk. Upon receiving the news of Seymour's decapitation, she had no discernible emotional reaction.

Following the death of the Protestant Edward in 1553 and the ascension of Elizabeth's elder half-sister Mary, who was fervently devoted to restoring England to the Roman Catholic religion, the need for caution, self-restraint, and political astuteness became even more crucial. This endeavour, in addition to her unfavourable union with the fervently Catholic monarch Philip II of Spain, incited vehement Protestant resistance. Elizabeth faced a significant threat to her life in an intense climate of traitorous revolt and inquisitorial persecution. Although she ostensibly adhered to official Catholic practises as her sister requested, she unavoidably became the central figure and the clear recipient of schemes to topple the government and reinstate Protestantism. Following Sir Thomas Wyatt's insurrection in January 1554, Elizabeth was apprehended and subsequently incarcerated in the Tower of London. However, she managed to barely escape, suffering the same fate as her mother. Following two months of thorough questioning and surveillance, which failed to uncover any definitive proof of her involvement in treasonous activities, she was subsequently freed from the Tower and sent to strict confinement at Woodstock for a duration of one year. Her predicament became considerably less challenging, but she was always under close and distrustful observation. During Mary's reign, which was marked by her inability to have children, persecution of Protestants, and military failures, Elizabeth consistently had to assert her innocence, declare her unshakable commitment, and express her strong disapproval of heresy. The experience was a continuous demonstration of how to endure and thrive by practising self-control and skillfully managing one's outward image.

# 24.

# SULEIMAN THE MAGNIFICENT (OTTOMAN EMPIRE)

Sultan Süleyman I of the Ottoman Empire (popularly known as "the Magnificent" in the West) took the oath of office in September 1520.

Far back when he was a youth, he was already serving as governor of a province and had a pivotal role in his father Selim's (r.1512-1520) uprising, which ultimately led to his own and Süleyman's accession to the throne.

The longest Ottoman rule ever was Süleyman's, which lasted 46 years. He became one of the most formidable kings in European history at that time, expanding his empire's borders and inspiring dread among his enemies.

Following his coronation as sultan, Süleyman ruled over an empire that extended from the Balkans to Anatolia, the Levant, and Egypt. Its territory grew to include a larger portion of Mesopotamia, North Africa, and Hungary under his rule.

During the first half-century, Süleyman conquered Rhodes and Belgrade. Also in 1526, he defeated the Hungarian kingdom and its allies in the Battle of Mohács, where King Louis the Second of Hungary (r. 1516–1526) died. The majority of Hungary fell under Ottoman control when a succession crisis and boundary dispute broke out upon his death among Habsburg Austria, the Ottomans, the Croatian and Hungarian kingdoms. Years down the road, in 1566, during his last war against Szigetvár, Hungary, Süleyman passed away "peacefully" in his command tent.

His dominion was home to people of many different faiths, languages, and ethnicities. Ottoman authorities were unconcerned with violently altering the ways of life of peaceful rural communities. Ottoman rule was therefore often limited by regional traditions. Authorities from the Ottoman Empire were believed to be well-versed in local customs and traditions, which they were instructed to respect and avoid upsetting.

During Süleyman's rule, there was a resurgence of concern for Islamic religious affairs, adding to Islam's favoured position in the Ottoman realm. Despite this, every ethnic group in the empire was able to find a place to call home and thrive under his rule.

For 46 years, Süleyman was the undisputed leader of Europe. He did not stop Protestantism from gaining hold in Hungary or Transylvania, and he even promised to help Protestant causes (such as undermining the Habsburgs) succeed. He turned a large portion of the Mediterranean into a "Ottoman lake" for decades after forming an alliance with the French to fight the Habsburgs. Even now, contemporary Europe shows the traces of Süleyman's rule.

Süleyman expanded his father's tentative claim to the Caliphate and Universal Rule inside the Islamic world. The subsequent Ottoman sultans considered themselves to be the "head" of all Sunni Muslims and the Caliph. Süleyman's assertion further solidified divisions between Shi'a and Sunni institutions, as the Shi'a Safavids (based in Persia) & the Sunni Ottomans fought to establish the legitimacy of their authority and assert their claims. The confessional issues and division between the two empires and sects were further exacerbated by this conflict.

# 25.

# ASHOKA (INDIA)

The last great ruler of the Indian Mauryan dynasty was Ashoka. Buddhism was actively promoted by him throughout his reign (c. 265-238 BCE; reported as c. 273-232 BCE), which contributed to its expansion to India. After violently conquering the eastern coast of India after his invasion of Kalinga, Ashoka gave up on military triumph in favour of "victory by dharma."

From 273 BC to 232 BC, during his reign, India had one of its most prosperous periods. Including vast swaths of India, South Asia, and beyond, the Ashoka empire reached from what is now Afghanistan and a portion of Persia in the west to eastern Bengal and Assam, and southern Mysore. Although he had a change of heart during the brutal War of Kalinga, Buddhist texts portray Ashoka as a cruel and merciless king. Upon returning from the war, he made a personal commitment to Buddhism and spent the rest of his life preaching its teachings.

He gained notoriety as a kind king who ordered his subjects to be given an equitable distribution of land. 'Devanampriya Priyadarshi' was bestowed upon him as a king due to his kind disposition. In recognition of his apolitical attitude, the Dharma Chakra that adorns the Ashok stambh is now a part of the Indian national flag. One of India's most prosperous periods was associated with Ashoka and his magnificent reign. A representation of the Indian Republic has been the Ashoka Lion Capital.

Oral proclamations and inscriptions on rocks and pillars in key places were how Ashoka spread his ideas and his work. The lion's capital at Sarnath, a symbol of the Indian subcontinent, is just one example of the many inscriptions carved into rock and pillar systems that were likely penned during the king's reign and include declarations detailing his ideas and deeds.

To get the word out about his ideas and activities, Ashoka would make vocal announcements and etch inscriptions on prominent pillars and rocky outcrops. Typically penned during the course of his reign, rock and pillar inscriptions (such as the lion's capital, discovered at Sarnath and now representing the Indian subcontinent) contain details about his life and statements of his views and deeds.

Public announcements of Ashoka's ideals and endeavours were made on rocks and pillars at key locations, both orally and in writing. Proclamations on his beliefs and activities, as well as details about his life and deeds (such as the lion's capital, which has been discovered in Sarnati), are carved into the rock and pillars throughout his reign.

His civic service included building hospitals for both humans and animals, landscaping the roadside with trees and bushes, excavating wells, and constructing irrigation centers and bathrooms. Animal abuse and public carelessness were also addressed via the issuance of orders. Following Ashoka's death, the Mauryan empire fell apart, and his endeavours were neglected. As a result of her aspirations and rigorous standards, her impact is being felt even now.

The care for the well-being of Ashoka's people grew in his administration after his spiritual awakening. The emperor governed over the nobility, as had been the practise from the time of the Mauryan kings before Ashoka. Before implementing any new administrative policy, Ashoka spoke with Vithashoka, his younger brother, and a group of trustworthy ministers who helped him out with his administrative tasks. Notable members of the advisory council were Yuvaraj, the

Prince of Crown, Mahamantri, the Prime Minister, Senapati, the General, and Purohita. During Asoka's reign, several improvements were made compared to his predecessors. He drew on his father's style of governance in response to Kalinga's choice, declaring, "All men are my children." Another thing he did was tell his slaves how much he loved and respected them, and how he felt driven to help them out.

# 26.

# BENITO MUSSOLINI (ITALY)

It was in the northern region of central Italy, between Bologna and Florence, that Benito Mussolini was born. His father was a blacksmith, while his mother was a kindergarten teacher. Mussolinli was a clever boy, but he was notorious for his rage and was responsible for stabbing two of his classmates while he was in school. After following in his mother's footsteps, he became a school master; nevertheless, he discovered that the work was not a suitable fit for him for some reason. Instead, he worked as an editor for a newspaper and then launched his own publication, which he called La Lotta di Classe (The Class Struggle). In this publication, he would publish his political and philosophical beliefs that were considered to be extremist. During the First World War, he participated in the military; however, he was forced to return home due to physical concerns and resume his work in the newspaper industry. Mussolini, who was dissatisfied with the way Italian politics were being conducted at the time, organised the Fascist party to march on Rome. He then exerted such substantial pressure on King Victor Emmanuel that he granted Mussolini the opportunity to seize control of the government and create a new one in 1922, making him the youngest Prime Minister of Italy in history. The year 1938 saw the beginning of Mussolini's implementation of anti-semitic legislation and beliefs, which he had associated himself with Hitler, the "Pact of Steel."

Between the invasion of Poland by Hitler and the beginning of the Second World War, Mussolini maintained his neutrality until 1940, when France was on the verge of collapse. As a result of Japan's bombing of Pearl Harbour, which brought the United States into the Second World War, Italy, Germany, and Japan came together to establish the Axis alliance. Due to the fact that the Italian military was relatively weak in comparison to the armed forces of the other nations involved in the war, Mussolini suffered a significant number of combat casualties. He was incarcerated in 1943 because he was no longer a viable leader at that point. It was in 1945 as he attempted to flee the Allied troops who were sweeping across Italy that he was taken captive and ultimately put to death.

# 27.

# THOMAS JEFFERSON (USA)

Thomas Jefferson, who was born on April 2 (April 13, New Style), 1743 in Shadwell, Virginia, and passed away on July 4, 1826 in Monticello, Virginia, was a draughtsman of the Declaration of Independence of the United States of America. He also served as the nation's first secretary of state (1789–94) and second vice president (1797–1801), and he was the statesman responsible for the Louisiana Purchase during his third term as president (1801–09). In addition to being an early supporter of the principle of complete separation of religion and state, he was also the founder and architect of the University of Virginia. He was arguably the most vocal American champion of individual liberty as the fundamental principle that underpinned the American Revolution.

Jefferson, who has been recognised for a long time as the most prominent "apostle of liberty" in the United States, has seen an increase in the amount of critical examination within the academic community. At the popular level, he continues to be an incandescent icon, an inspirational symbol for both major political parties in the

United States, as well as for dissenters in communist China, liberal reformers in central and eastern Europe, and aspiring democrats in Africa and Latin America. This is true both in the United States and abroad. His reputation, on the other hand, has deteriorated as a result of the increased attention paid to racial equality, which has led to a more pessimistic reevaluation of his reliance on slavery and his belief that American society continues to be the authority of white men. The DNA findings of the investigation that was conducted in 1998 revealed that Jefferson had virtually likely been the father of a child with his slave Sally Hemings, who was thirty years his younger. This revelation was very upsetting to a lot of people. Jefferson is now considered to be the most troublesome and contradictory hero in the United States of America due to the significant disparity that exists between his poetic presentation of liberal ideas and the more subdued reality of his own life. On the occasion of the two hundredth anniversary of his birth, on April 13, 1943, the Jefferson Memorial in Washington, District of Columbia, was dedicated to him.

# 28.

# INDIRA GANDHI (INDIA)

Indian politician Indira Gandhi was the country's first female prime minister, holding the office for four years (from 1980 until her assassination in 1984). She was born on November 19, 1917, in Allahabad, India, and died on October 31, 1984, in New Delhi.

Jawaharlal Nehru was a formidable figure in India's fight for independence from Britain. His only child, Indira Nehru, was prime minister of independent India from 1947 to 1964. Jawaharlal was also a prominent leader of the influential and long-dominant Indian National Congress (Congress Party). Her grandpa Motilal Nehru was an ally of Mahatma Gandhi and an early leader in the freedom struggle. She spent a year at the University of Oxford in England and another year at Visva-Bharati University in Shantiniketan (now Bolpur, West Bengal state). In 1938, she became a member of the Congress Party.

She got married party member Feroze Gandhi (who passed away in 1960) in 1942. The couple's offspring included Rajiv and Sanjay.

Despite this, the parents spent a significant amount of time apart throughout their marriage. After her mother passed away in the mid-1930s, Indira often took up the role of hostess for her father's social gatherings and travelled beside him on his adventures.

Pictured here in March 1962 in New Delhi, India, are Indira Gandhi (far left) and Jacqueline Kennedy (far right), the first lady of the United States of America.

In 1947, Gandhi's father became the president of the Congress Party, and in 1955, Gandhi joined the party's working committee. The role of party president, which is mostly ceremonial, was voted to her in 1959. In 1964, she became a member of the Rajya Sabha, the upper house of India's parliament. In the same year, her minister of information and broadcasting was chosen by Lal Bahadur Shastri, who had replaced Nehru as prime minister.

As a result of a compromise between the conservative and liberal factions of the Congress Party, Gandhi was designated as party leader and prime minister upon Shastri's unexpected death in January 1966. Nevertheless, the conservative faction of the party, spearheaded by the late Morarji Desai, persistently questioned her leadership. In 1967, Gandhi accepted Desai's position as deputy prime minister after she was elected to the Lok Sabha, the lower house of India's parliament, on the Congress Party's ticket. However, the party's majority was so narrow that Gandhi had to concede defeat.

But in 1969, she was booted out of the party by Desai and the other old guard as tensions rose inside. Gandhi remained unfazed and rallied the support of most of her party members to establish a new group known as the "New" Congress Party. Despite facing opposition from a coalition of conservative parties, the New Congress party emerged victorious in the 1971 Lok Sabha elections. In late 1971, when East Pakistan (now Bangladesh) was fighting for independence from Pakistan, Gandhi was a major supporter of the independence movement. As a result, India's military forces defeated Pakistan in a short and decisive war, and Bangladesh was born. She made history by recognising the new nation before any other government official.

The country's triumph against Pakistan in March 1972 gave Gandhi and her New Congress Party faction a boost, and they won a slew of state legislative assembly elections in March 1972. Her 1971 national election opponent from the Socialist Party, who she had beaten, soon after that filed charges that she had broken election laws in that race. A ruling against her from the High Court of Allahabad in June 1975 meant that she would lose her parliamentary seat and be barred from politics for six years. The Supreme Court did not respond satisfactorily to her appeal of the decision. By herself, she took things into her own hands, imposing a nationwide state of emergency in India, locking up her political rivals, and assuming emergency powers. Individual liberties were curtailed by a plethora of newly passed statutes. During that time, she also instituted a number of controversial policies, such as widespread sterilisation to control the population.

# 29.

# CHARLEMAGNE (FRANKISH EMPIRE)

Charlemagne, born on April 2, 747 (exact date uncertain) and died on January 28, 814 at Aachen, Austrasia (now in Germany), was the king of the Franks from 768 to 814. He also served as the king of the Lombards from 774 to 814 and became the first emperor of the Romans and the Holy Roman Empire from 800 to 814.

During the approximate period of Charlemagne's birth, which is often believed to be in 742 but more likely to be in 747 or 748, his father, Pippin III (also known as "the Short"), held the position of mayor of the palace. This role included serving the Merovingian monarch, but in reality, Pippin III maintained significant control over the vast Frankish empire. Scant information on Charlemagne's early life indicates that he acquired practical skills for leadership by active involvement in the political, social, and military affairs of his father's court. The first period of his life was characterised by a series of occurrences that had significant consequences for the Frankish influence on the present-day global landscape. In 751, Pippin, with the endorsement of the Pope, took control of the Frankish monarchy from Childeric III, the last ruler of the Merovingian dynasty. Following a meeting with Pope Stephen II at the royal palace of Ponthion in 753–754, Pippin established a partnership with the pope by pledging to defend Rome in exchange for papal approval of his dynasty's claim to the Frankish crown. Pippin also took military action in Italy in 755 and 756 to counter Lombard threats towards Rome. In 756, he made the Donation of Pippin, granting the papacy a significant portion of land in central Italy. This territory became the foundation of a new political entity known as the Papal States, which were under the rule of the pope.

Upon Pippin's death in 768, his kingdom was partitioned in accordance with Frankish tradition between Charlemagne and his brother, Carloman. The rivalry between the two brothers posed an immediate danger to the cohesion of the Frankish monarchy. In order to gain an edge over his brother, Charlemagne created a partnership with Desiderius, the king of the Lombards. As part of this deal, Charlemagne married the daughter of the Lombard king, which posed a danger to the fragile balance that had been achieved in Italy via Pippin's alliance with the pope. Carloman's death in 771 resolved the escalating situation, allowing Charlemagne to seize full control of the Frankish kingdom, without respect for the rights of Carloman's successors.

# 30.

# ANGELA MERKEL (GERMANY)

Angela Merkel is a German politician who was chancellor of Germany from 2005 to 2021. She was born on July 17, 1954, in Hamburg, West Germany. Among Germany's chancellors, she had the second-longest tenure and was the first woman to do so.

Merkel was born to Horst Kasner, a theology student, and Herlind Kasner, a Latin and English teacher, in Hamburg. Shortly after Merkel was born, her family moved to East Germany (now the German Democratic Republic) because her father had taken a pastorate in Quitzow, Brandenburg, after finishing his schooling. After relocating to Templin in 1957, Merkel completed high school there in 1973. She enrolled at the University of Leipzig (formerly Karl Marx University) in Leipzig, Germany, to study physics later that year. She wed Ulrich Merkel, a fellow physics student, in 1977 after meeting him there. She became an academic faculty member at the Central Institute of Physical Chemistry of the Academy of Sciences in East Berlin after receiving her graduation in 1978. Merkel retained her husband's surname during their 1982 divorce. In 1986, she received a doctoral degree for her work in quantum chemistry.

Merkel was an active member of the state's youth groups, as were the majority of youngsters in the German Democratic Republic throughout her childhood. From 1962 to 1968, she was an active member of both the Young Pioneers and the Free German Youth. There has been some controversy surrounding her involvement with the Free German Youth. Her former coworkers at the Central Institute of Physical Chemistry asserted that she was the institute's secretary for agitation and propaganda, but Merkel insisted that her responsibilities included cultural affairs, such as acquiring theatre tickets. Merkel declined an offer from members of the Stasi to become an informant and was never a member of the Socialist Unity Party, neither of which she applied for.

Merkel became the press spokeswoman for the newly formed Democratic Awakening in February 1990 after joining the party when the Berlin Wall fell in 1989. The party became a member of the conservative Alliance for Germany that same month, which was a coalition with the Christian Democratic Union (CDU), the German Social Union (DSU), and the state. In March 1990, just days before East Germany's first and only free election, it was made public that Wolfgang Schnur, chairman of the Democratic Awakening, had spent years as an informant for the Stasi. In spite of the fact that the news rocked Alliance supporters, the coalition prevailed, and Democratic Awakening joined the government with just 0.9% of the vote. Merkel is now Lothar de Maizière's (CDU) deputy spokesperson. In August of 1990, she became a member of the CDU; the day before Germany's reunification, on October 1, the CDU united with its western equivalent.

# 31.

# AUGUSTUS CAESAR (ROME)

Caesar Augustus, also known as Gaius Octavius later Gaius Julius Caesar Octavianus, was the first Roman Emperor during his reign. He was born on September 23, 63 BC, and passed away on August 19, AD 14, at Nola, which is located near Naples. When he was 18 years old, he was given the title of adopted son and heir to his great-uncle Julius Caesar. He was born into a rich family. Following the killing of Caesar in 44 BC, a power struggle erupted, and after a number of conflicts, Octavian founded the Second Triumvirate with his most significant adversaries, Lepidus and Mark Antony. To establish himself as the only ruler, Octavian defeated Lepidus in the year 32 and Antony, who was at the time allied with Cleopatra, in the Battle of Actium in the year 31. Although he was crowned princeps, it is believed that his ascension marked the beginning of the Roman Empire.

His first position was that of a consul, during which he maintained republican governance. However, in the year 27, he took the title of Augustus, and in the year 23, he was granted imperial authority.

During his reign, which lasted from 31 BC to 14 AD, improvements were made to every facet of Roman life, and the Greco-Roman world saw enduring peace and prosperity. In addition to establishing the Pax Romana and fostering the arts, he was responsible for the protection of remote imperial provinces, highways, and public works. As part of his efforts to restore Roman virtue, he ordered the exile of his daughter Julia, who had committed adultery. The empire included a territory that extended from Iberia to Cappadocia as well as from Gaul to Egypt until he passed away. After his death, he was deified as a god.

# 32.

# JOHN F. KENNEDY (USA)

As his motorcade passed through Dallas, Texas, on November 22, 1963—just over a thousand days into his presidency—John Fitzgerald Kennedy was shot and murdered. Not only was John F. Kennedy the youngest president to have be elected, but he also died at that age.

His birthplace was Brookline, Massachusetts, and he was born on May 29, 1917. His family was Irish. After finishing Harvard in 1940, he enlisted in the Navy. Despite suffering serious injuries, Kennedy guided the survivors of his PT boat that had been struck and destroyed by a Japanese ship in 1943 to safety, navigating them across treacherous seas.

After serving his country, he returned to the Boston area and ran for Congress as a Democrat. In 1953, he was elected to the Senate. On the 12th of September, 1953, he wed Jacqueline Bouvier. While he was in the hospital recovering from back surgery in 1955, he penned the Pulitzer Prize–winning biography Profiles in Courage.

Kennedy was a first-ballot candidate for president four years after coming close to receiving the Democratic selection for vice president in 1956. His debates with Richard M. Nixon, the Republican candidate, were seen by millions of people on television. After becoming the first Roman Catholic president, Kennedy won the popular vote by a razor-thin margin.

"Ask not what your country can do for you-ask what you can do for your country." That was the unforgettable admonition he issued in his inaugural address. Redeeming his campaign promise to get America rolling again was his first order of business as president. Before he passed away, he devised a strategy to attack persistent areas of poverty and hardship on a vast scale, and his economic programmes set the nation on its longest continuous growth since WWII.

In response to mounting calls for immediate action, he vigorously pursued equal rights and advocated for new civil rights laws. The importance of the arts to a thriving society and the high quality of American culture were also important to him as he envisioned America.

He hoped the United States will return to its roots as the pioneer in the fight for human rights. Through his work with the Peace Corps and the Alliance for Progress, he mobilised American idealism to support underdeveloped countries. However, the Communist threat remained a harsh reality.

Kennedy authorised the invasion of Cuba by a group of armed and trained Cuban exiles not long after he took office. It was not possible to topple Fidel Castro's government. Almost immediately after that, the Soviet Union escalated its offensive on West Berlin once more. In response, Kennedy increased the nation's military might and sent reinforcements to the Berlin garrison, among other things, to launch new space missions. In response to this backlash, Moscow eased sanctions on central Europe after the Berlin Wall's construction.

Russian plans shifted to include deploying nuclear missiles to Cuba. Air surveillance revealed this in October 1962, and Kennedy promptly quarantined all offensive weaponry destined for Cuba. Russia eventually decided to remove the missiles as the world teetered on the edge of nuclear Armageddon. Evidently, Moscow was convinced that nuclear blackmail was pointless after the United States' reaction to the Cuban crisis.

In his 1963 test prohibition agreement, Kennedy argued that halting the proliferation of nuclear weapons while decreasing the pace of the arms race were critical interests of both the United States and Russia. Towards his vision of "a world of law and free choice, banishing the world of war and coercion," there was substantial improvement in the months after the Cuban crisis. Thus, fresh optimism for American equality and global peace began during his presidency.

# 33.

# CATHERINE THE GREAT (RUSSIA)

Empress regent of Russia from 1762 until 1796 was Catherine II of Russia, often known as Catherine the Great. Their aristocratic but impoverished family was brought into this world in Prussia by Prince Christian August of Anhalt-Zerbst (1690–1747) and Princess Johanna Elisabeth of Holstein–Gottorp (1712–1760). at 1745, at St. Petersburg, she wed Peter of Holstein-Gottorp, who would later become a Russian tsar (1728–1762).

By 1762, Peter had become Russia's Emperor Peter III, and Catherine had become his empress consort. Unfortunately, Catherine came to despise Peter and everything he stood for throughout their unhappy marriage and shared rule. Catherine wasted no time in trying to depose Peter and finding assistance elsewhere. Her allies in the Russian army had Peter imprisoned and made to sign an abdication document. Not long after that, he was shot dead, making Catherine the only ruler of Russia.

On September 22, 1762, Catherine was officially crowned Catherine II of Russia, becoming the empress regent. She brought about the Russian Enlightenment by transforming the country's educational system, culture, and economy throughout her long reign.

In 1729, Sophie Friederike Auguste von Anhalt-Zerbst-Dornburg was born to Christian August, Prince of Anhalt-Zerbst and Princess Johanna Elisabeth of Holstein-Gottorp in Stettin, Prussia (now known as Szczecin, Poland). There was a younger sister and two younger brothers in her family. Wound up with scarlet fever at the tender age of twelve, Wilhem Christian was one of her younger brothers. Apparently, Catherine was more connected to her dad than her mom.

Despite their financial struggles, Catherine received the education befitting a child of aristocratic origin from a French governess and tutors. Elizabeth (Babet) Cardel, Catherine's governess, had a profound impact on her; in fact, Catherine said that Elizabeth was the ideal governess. Catherine has boundless vitality and an infectious smile. She liked leading games and activities with the local kids. Catherine says her upbringing was rather dull, with "nothing of interest in it."

# 34.

# DWIGHT D. EISENHOWER (USA)

During his two years as president, Dwight D. Eisenhower did an incredible job of easing tensions between the Cold War and the Soviet Union, using his status as the commanding general of the victorious troops in Europe during WWII. He also succeeded in obtaining a ceasefire in Korea. "America is today the strongest, most influential and most productive nation in the world, "he said as he stepped down from office, praising the moderate policies of "Modern Republicanism."

Eisenhower was the third of seven boys; he was born in Texas in 1890 and raised in Abilene, Kansas. He was chosen to West Point because of his outstanding athletic performance in high school. He wed Mamie Geneva Doud in 1916 while stationed in Texas as a second lieutenant.

While working under Generals John J. Pershing, Douglas MacArthur, and Walter Krueger, he was an outstanding staff officer in the early stages of his Army career. Following Pearl Harbour, he was summoned to Washington, DC, by General George C. Marshall to be assigned the task of war planning. On D-Day, 1944, he oversaw the invasion of France as Supreme Commander, and in November 1942, he oversaw the Allied Forces' arrival in North Africa.

He served as president of Columbia University after the war ended, but in 1951 he stepped down to become supreme commander of the newly formed NATO troops. Envoys from the Republican Party convinced him to seek the presidency in 1952 at his headquarters in Paris.

A rallying cry of "I like Ike" helped Eisenhower to a decisive victory.

In an effort to defuse the Cold War, he negotiated based on military might. An armistice was signed in 1953, bringing about a ceasefire along the South Korean border. Relations with Russia changed after Stalin's death that year.

A peace pact that neutralised Austria was approved upon by the new Russian government. At the same time, hydrogen bombs were being researched by both Russia and the US. In July 1955, Eisenhower convened a summit in Geneva with the heads of state from the United Kingdom, France, and Russia in the face of the global danger posed by this devastating power.

In his State of the Union address, President Trump suggested that Russia and the US share plans for their respective military installations and "provide within our countries facilities for aerial photography to the other country." Although the Russians remained silent in response to the idea, they were very kind throughout the sessions, which helped to ease tensions.

During a visit to Denver, Colorado, in September 1955, Eisenhower had an abrupt heart attack. He was discharged from the hospital after seven weeks, and his recovery was announced by physicians in February 1956. He was re-elected to a second term in November.

When it came to domestic policy, the president took a moderate approach, maintaining a balanced budget but keeping most programmes from the New Deal and the Fair Deal. In the midst of school desegregation, he dispatched soldiers to Little Rock, Arkansas, to enforce a federal court's orders and to desegregate the military as a whole. "This nation must not tolerate any kind of second-class citizen," he said in his letter.

Keeping the peace across the globe was Eisenhower's top priority. He relished seeing his "atoms for peace" initiative, which included the peaceful loan of uranium from the United States to countries that "have not," come to fruition.

Prior to his January 1961 departure for his Gettysburg farm, he stressed the need of keeping a sufficient military force, but warned that massive, sustained military spending might pose threats to our way of life. A plea for peace was his last words, said "in the goodness of time." Upon his death on March 28, 1969, after a protracted illness, these subjects were still relevant and pressing.

35.

# RAMSES II (EGYPT)

The third pharaoh of ancient Egypt's 19th dynasty, Ramses II (died 13th century BCE), had the second-longest reign in Egyptian history (1279-13 BCE). Along with his conflicts with the Hittites and the Libyans, he is commemorated in Egypt by several monumental sculptures of himself and his vast construction projects. The nonroyal Ramses family ascended to power a few decades following the religious reformer Akhenaton's (Amenhotep IV, 1353–36 BCE) rule and began to reestablish Egyptian dominance in Asia, which had diminished during Akhenaton's and Tutankhamen's reigns. Seti I, father of Ramses, crushed the rebellions of many princes in southern Syria and Palestine and went to war with the Hittites of Anatolia to reclaim the northern regions that had fallen under Hittite rule during the last upheaval. In the beginning, Seti had some success against the Hittites. However, his victories were short-lived since by the time he died, the Hittites had taken Kadesh, a stronghold on the Orontes River that was strategically important to their southern boundary.

The future Ramses II, crown prince Ramses, was granted special regent status during Seti's reign. Seti gave him a harem and a royal household, and the young prince went on wars with his father, so he was well-prepared for the role of single ruler. Ramses' extremely early designation as heir raises eyebrows; it's almost as if it were a guarantee that he would really take the throne. Although he may have been undergoing military training at the time, his title as captain of the army at the tender age of ten was almost certainly honorary.

Constructed on a grand scale, the city of Per Ramessu ("House of Ramses"; biblical Raamses) was renowned for its picturesque design, featuring gardens, orchards, and pleasant waters. Ramses lived there because his family's home was in the Nile River delta, so he needed a convenient base for campaigns in Asia. In the west, the goddess Amon presided; in the south, Seth; in the north, Wadjet, the royal cobra goddess; and, most importantly, in the east, the Syrian goddess Astarte. A trend towards Asian gods had begun in Egypt, as well as Ramses himself had strong preferences in that direction.

Upon becoming sole ruler, Ramses' first public act was to go to Thebes, the capital of the southern kingdom, to attend the major religious festival of Opet, during which the deity Amon of Karnak paid a state visit to the Temple of Luxor on his ceremonial barge. The northern monarch stopped in Abydos on his way back to his home to worship Osiris as well as resume construction on the huge temple his father had constructed there; the previous king's death had halted the project. Nebwenenef, who had previously served as high priest of Anhur at the neighbouring temple of Thinis, was also appointed by him to become the new high priest of Amon at Thebes.

# 36.

# RONALD REAGAN (USA)

Ronald Wilson Reagan was born February 6, 1911, in Tampico, Illinois. Father Jack was a failing businessman and drinker; mother Nelle was kind and devout. Reagan praised Dixon, a tiny midwestern town, as "a place where life was wholesome...people trusted each other, and nobody locked his door at night." Reagan was a lifeguard at the Rock River beach for seven summers as a youngster, saving 77 lives. Reagan maintained this hero image throughout his life. Reagan biographer Edmund Morris called the Rock River "the central symbol of his youth."

Reagan excelled in football and school plays during his four years at Eureka College, but not academically. In 1932, he graduated amid the Depression. The "Great Communicator" became a sportscaster for an Iowa radio station after six weeks.

Hollywood hosted Ronald Reagan in 1937. Under contract to Warner Brothers, he was often cast as himself or a near version. He debuted as a radio broadcaster in Love Is on the Air. His roles required him to be wholesome, Midwestern, and heroic. Reagan became famous for playing football hero George Gipp in Knute Rockne, All American and Drake McHugh in Kings Row after years as a "B" actor.

He excelled as Ronald Reagan. Reagan and Jane Wyman, married in 1940, appeared in Hollywood's innocence campaign. After America joined the war, Reagan left Wyman and newborn daughter Maureen in Los Angeles to serve in the Army Air Force Motion Picture Unit in Culver City, 19 miles away. Michael was adopted in 1946. Captain Reagan appeared in inspiring tales and training films here. He led America similarly 40 years later.

Reagan "returned" to Hollywood after the war and joined the SAG. From 1947 to 1952 and 1959 to 1960, he was SAG president five times. Reagan appeared before the House Committee on Un-American Activities in 1946 during the Hollywood Red Scare as a "friendly" witness without naming names. Reagan gained his anti-Communist sentiments from fighting SAG's claimed Communist infiltration, which he held throughout his administration.

Reagan's marriage and film career failed after the war. Reagan and Wyman divorced 1949. He remarried 1952. Reagan and Nancy Davis had two children, Patti and Ron, and one of Hollywood's most successful marriages. As adults, Patti and Ron would explain that their parents' love contrasted with their emotional distance from their children.

Reagan hosted G.E. Theatre in 1952. As business representative, the registered Democrat became a conservative spokesman at factory stops nationwide. He switched parties in 1962 and stunned the country in 1964 by speaking for conservative republican presidential nominee Barry Goldwater.

Reagan ran for governor of California in 1966. Reagan said during his campaign, "I don't know; I've never played a governor." Reagan was reelected governor of California after promising to lower property taxes, minimise government waste, and calm Berkeley students. He won support for his Welfare Reform Bill in his second term. The California State Assembly passed a law that decreased welfare overuse and reflected "some of the key themes of Reagan's conservative philosophy."

Some of Reagan's governorship activities appear odd given his conservative presidency. Reagan signed abortion-friendly legislation.

Although he considered homosexuality "an abomination" religiously, he was hesitant to condemn people. Later, in 1978, he opposed California's Briggs initiative, which would ban gay teachers. The proposal failed.

Reagan was elected president in 1980 on a platform of "a new consensus with all those across the land who share a community of values embodied in these words: family, work, neighbourhood, peace and freedom." He pledged to resist Communism, minimise government involvement in the economy, and boost national pride. He stole Knute Rockne's phrase to rally support for his agenda: "win one for the Gipper."

Reagan was called the "Teflon president," his popularity unaffected by performance. Teflon wasn't always reliable. Reagan's optimism faded throughout the 1982 recession, especially for the nine million jobless by November. His approval dropped to 35%. Only a strong 1983 economy revived Reagan's popularity. During the Iran-Contra Scandal, just 14% of Americans believed the president that he had not swapped guns for hostages.

Reagan hated nuclear weapons but felt America should be fully prepared for a battle that should never happen. At peak military buildup, the Pentagon spent $34 billion per hour on munitions. He concluded his defence programme with the Strategic Defence Initiative. Though criticised as "Star Wars," Reagan felt a space defence system might protect America from nuclear catastrophe.

Reagan supported Solidarity in Poland, the Muhajaddin in Afghanistan, and the Contras in Nicaragua in his fight against communism. The 1983 Grenada invasion and Iran-Contra crisis resulted from this effort.

Reagan's worst phase began with Iran-Contra. Reagan began selling weapons to Iran for hostages in 1985, breaking the law and Reagan's commitment not to engage with terrorists. Reagan said he had not swapped weaponry for Lebanon hostages held by Iran's Ayatollah Khomeini, but the nation didn't believe him. The controversy intensified when sales proceeds were routed to the Contras in Nicaragua, violating the Boland Amendment. There was impeachment discussion. Reagan was never directly linked to the cash diversion, but his reputation was harmed when the country learned of his detachment from White House operations.

In the end, most Americans forgave Reagan for Iran-Contra, and his Summit discussions with Mikhail Gorbachev restored his reputation. Reagan departed office with record-low unemployment and a growing economy, masking government's fiscal imbalances. His supporters continue to credit his military buildup and personal drive with ending Communism, often at the cost of Gorbachev. Reagan dubbed the Cold War's conclusion a "triumph of democracy."

Reagan's popular image remains bright. After he acknowledged in 1994 that he had Alzheimer's, fears grew that the illness had taken root in government; his capacity to focus and absorb information had been questioned. Not a problem. Reagan was strong, cheerful, and American on film and in politics.

# 37.

# EMPEROR MEIJI (JAPAN)

Meiji, who was born on November 3, 1852 in Kyōto and passed away on July 30, 1912 in Tokyo, was the Emperor of Japan from 1867 to 1912. During his reign, Japan saw a remarkable transformation, transitioning from a feudal realm to becoming one of the most powerful nations in the contemporary world.

Mutsuhito, the second son of Emperor Kōmei, was elevated to the position of crown prince in the year 1860. This was after his father passed away in the year 1867, which led to his elevation to the throne. His coronation ceremony took place in 1868, and he was given the name Meiji, which is also the term that is used to refer to the period of time during which he reigned. The fall of the Tokugawa shogunate and the restoration of supreme executive power in the nation to the emperor occurred simultaneously with Meiji's ascension to the throne of Japan. In contrast to Kōmei, he adhered to the emerging public consensus on the need of Japan's modernization along Western lines. This agreement had emerged as a consequence of Japan's return of contact with other countries after a period of cultural and economic isolation that lasted for 250 years. It was in the year 1868 that Meiji took the "Charter Oath of Five Principles," which was the first step in Japan's journey towards westernisation. As Emperor, he officially ordered the elimination of the feudal land system in 1871, the establishment of a new school system in 1872, the adoption of the cabinet system of government in 1885, the publication of the Meiji Constitution in 1889, and the inauguration of the Diet in 1890. However, he did not start any of these events. Within the context of the Sino-Japanese War (1894–95) or the Russo-Japanese War (1904–05), he was an active participant in the prosecution of both wars. The annexation of Korea to Japan was announced by an order that he issued in the year 1910.

Meiji himself exemplified the superimposition of Western ideas and inventions upon a foundation of Japanese culture. He dressed in Western attire and ate cuisine that was Western-style, yet he also managed to create 100,000 poems in the traditional Japanese style throughout his lifetime.

# 38.

# HO CHI MINH (VIETNAM)

Ho Chi Minh was president of the Democratic Republic of Vietnam (North Vietnam) from 1945 to 1969. He was born on May 19, 1890, in Hoang Tru, Vietnam, French Indochina, and died on September 2, 1969, in Hanoi, North Vietnam. Minh founded the Indochina Communist Party in 1930 and the Viet-Minh in 1941. Ho was a prominent figure in the anti-colonial struggle in Asia after WWII and a prominent communist leader of the twentieth century. He led the Vietnamese nationalist movement for over 30 years.

Kim Lien was the place where Ho Chi Minh was raised by his impoverished father, Nguyen Sinh Huy, a rural scholar. Despite his troubled upbringing, he managed to attend a Hue grammar school from the years 14 to 18. After that, he served as an instructor at a Phan Thiet school and then an apprentice at a Saigon technical college.

Working as a chef aboard a French steamboat in 1911, he went by the moniker Ba. He spent almost three years at sea, sailing to ports in Africa and the United States (specifically, Boston and New York). He lived in London from 1915 to 1917 and then relocated to France, where he had a series of odd jobs included gardening, cleaning, waiting tables, picture editing, and stoking ovens.

While he was a socialist in France from 1917 until 1923, he went by the moniker Nguyen Ai Quoc ("Nguyen the Patriot"). He rallied the local Vietnamese population and presented an eight-point petition to the delegates of the world's leading nations at the 1919 Versailles Peace Conference, which officially ended World War I. Ho pleaded with the French colonial authorities to treat the Indochina people fairly in his appeal. Although the peacemakers did not react to this, he became a hero to many politically aware Vietnamese. After the French Socialists resigned from the party in December 1920, Ho became a member of the French Communists, influenced by Vladimir Lenin's anti-imperialist ideology and the Russian communist revolution's triumph the previous year.

At the tail end of 1923, Ho travelled to Moscow after his years of militant involvement in France, during which he got familiar with the majority of the French working-class leaders. He offered a touching eulogy to the Soviet Union's founder in Pravda in January 1924, after Lenin's death. At the Fifth Congress of the Communist International, which he attended six months later (June 17–July 8), he voiced his disapproval of the French Communist Party's lack of stance against colonialism. Notable for including his first conviction in the revolutionary role of downtrodden peasants (rather than industrial workers), his speech to the congress is worth mentioning.

The Vietnam Thanh Nien Cach Menh Dong Chi Hoi ("Vietnamese Revolutionary Youth Association"), better known as Thanh Nien, was founded in December 1924 when Ho travelled to Canton (Guangzhou), a communist stronghold, in December 1924, using the alias Ly Thuy. He recruited the initial cadres of the Vietnamese nationalist movement and organised them into this group. Its members had banded together to fight French colonisation of Indochina; almost all of them had been deported from the nation due to their political views. Therefore, Indochinese nationalism originated in Canton.

Once again, Ho sought sanctuary in the Soviet Union after Chiang Kai-shek, the then-commander of the Chinese army, ousted the Chinese communists from Canton in April 1927. Before travelling to

Siam (now Thailand) in 1928, he visited Brussels and Paris. After that, he spent two years in Southeast Asia representing the Communist International, a global organisation of communist parties. But his disciples stuck around in southern China.

# 39.

# WOODROW WILSON (USA)

American politician and academic Woodrow Wilson, who was born on December 28, 1856, in Staunton, Virginia, U.S., and died on February 3, 1924, in Washington, D.C., was the 28th president of the United States (1913–1921). He is most known for his achievements in legislation and his idealistic, progressive outlook. Wilson won the Nobel Peace Prize in 1919 for guiding the United States into World War I and for establishing and championing the League of Nations. During his second time in office, the United States Constitution was amended to include a provision granting women the franchise. The worst crisis of presidential infirmity in American history occurred when he had a paralytic stroke in October 1919, when he was trying to rally popular support for the Treaty of Versailles in the United States. His incapacity persisted throughout his remaining tenure in office.

The father of Wilson, Joseph Ruggles Wilson, was a Presbyterian pastor who had emigrated to Virginia from Ohio; Janet Woodrow, the mother, was born in England to Scotch-Irish parents; and the father, Joseph, was the son of Scotch-Irish immigrants. Having a father born outside of the United States made Wilson the first president to do so since Andrew Jackson.

As one might expect, "Tommy" Wilson's childhood was heavily influenced by the Presbyterian church. As a result of his father's teaching and pastorates in Augusta, Georgia, and Wilmington, North Carolina, the family left Virginia before he turned two years old. He was educated at South Carolina's Columbia Theological Seminary. The young man decided to abandon his first name after college to emphasise the family link and because he believed "Woodrow Wilson" sounded more dignified. His uncle, James Woodrow, was the main light of the seminary faculty. His father was a clergyman for the Confederate forces in the Civil War, and his Augusta church became a military hospital. The atrocities of war had a profound effect on young Wilson.

Wilson, who was apparently dyslexic from a young age, struggled to read and did not develop reading speed until beyond the age of 10. But he became quite interested in literature and politics. He spent a year at Davidson College, close to Charlotte, North Carolina, before enrolling in Princeton University in 1875. Reading extensively, debating often, and managing the Princeton student newspaper all contributed to his intellectual blossoming while at Princeton. An academic article he produced as an undergraduate contrasted the American and British parliamentary systems of governance; he would expand on this theme in his first book and use it throughout his political career.

Wilson attended the University of Virginia School of Law after graduating from Princeton in 1879, thinking that a career in law would bring him into politics. After two years of dull law practise in Atlanta, he became disillusioned with the legal profession and decided to pursue doctoral studies in history and government at Johns Hopkins University. He became the only president to get a Ph.D. in 1886.

In Congressional Government: A Study in American Politics (1885), which served as both his dissertation and first book, Wilson expanded on his earlier comparisons between American and parliamentary governments and proposed changes that would make the former more effective and responsive to public opinion. One of Wilson's later works is Constitutional Government in the United States (1908), in which he deftly lays out the contemporary understanding of the president as "the representative of no constituency, but of the whole people." Other works by him include The State: Elements of Historical and Practical Politics (1889), a history of the United States, Division and Reunion, 1829–1889 (1893), the five-volume A History of the American People (1902), and more. His genuine nature shines through when he talks without ulterior motives.

# 40.

# RICHARD I (UK)

Richard I, born on September 8, 1157 and died on April 6, 1199, servedasthemonarchofEnglandfrom 1189 until his death. In addition, he held the titles of Duke of Normandy, Aquitaine, and Gascony, Lord of Cyprus, Count of Poitiers, Anjou, Maine, and Nantes, and exercised authority over Brittany at different points over that timeframe. He was the third son among five offspring of King Henry II of England and Duchess Eleanor of Aquitaine. Despite initially seeming improbable to ascend to the throne, all of his brothers, save the youngest, John, passed away before their father. Richard is often referred to as Richard Coeur de Lion (Norman French: Le quor de lion) or Richard the Lionheart due to his esteemed status as a formidable military commander and warrior. Bertran de Born, the troubadour, also referred to him as Richard Oc-e-Non, which translates to "Yes and No" in Occitan, probably because to his penchant for brevity.

At the age of 16, Richard assumed leadership of his own military force and successfully suppressed rebellions in Poitou against his father. Richard, a prominent Christian commander during the Third Crusade, assumed leadership of the campaign following the departure of Philip II of France. He achieved significant triumphs against his Muslim adversary, Saladin, but ultimately concluded a peace treaty and concluded the campaign without recapturing Jerusalem.

It is probable that Richard was proficient in both French and Occitan. He was born in England and spent his youth there. However, for the most of his adult life, he resided in the Duchy of Aquitaine, located in the southwest of France, before ascending to the throne. After assuming power, he allocated a minimal amount of time, maybe as little as six months, in England. The majority of his reign as monarch was dedicated to participating in Crusades, being held captive, or vigorously protecting his territories in France. Instead of seeing his kingdom as a duty that necessitates his presence as a monarch, he has been seen as choosing to view it just as a means of generating income to sustain his army. However, his people saw him as a devout hero. He is one of the few kings of England who is popularly known by his nickname rather than his specific reign number. He continues to be a prominent and influential person in both England and France.

# 41.

# HARRY S. TRUMAN (USA)

Harry S. Truman was the 33rd president of the United States (1945–1953). He was born May 8, 1884, in Lamar, Missouri, U.S., and died December 26, 1972, in Kansas City, Missouri. During his presidency, America fiercely opposed Soviet expansionism in Europe and the Soviet invasion of South Korea was repelled by U.S. forces.

As a farmer and mule dealer, Truman's father, John A., was the firstborn of three children born to Martha E. and John A. Truman. He began his career as a bank teller in Kansas City after finishing high school in Independence, Missouri, in 1901. He relocated to the farm in Grandview in 1906 and succeeded his father as farm manager upon his death in 1914. Having served two tours in the National Guard (1905–2011) and being almost 33 years old when America joined World War I in 1917, Truman promptly offered his services as a volunteer. His next posting was to France, where he oversaw the field artillery unit Battery D, which saw action at Saint Mihiel and the Meuse-Argonne. He was deployed abroad a year later. His troops were loyal to him since they looked up to him as a leader because of his courage and fairness.

After Truman returned to the US in 1919, he wed a boyhood friend, Elizabeth Wallace (Bess Truman); they had a daughter, Margaret, in 1924. He started a haberdashery with his army buddy Edward Jacobson, but they both went bankrupt during the devastating economic downturn of the early 1920s. He met Democratic Kansas City chairman Thomas Pendergast via another army buddy. Truman began his political career in 1922 when he ran for county judge and was successfully supported by the Pendergast machine. Although he was unsuccessful in his reelection attempt in 1924, he was re-elected as the county court's presiding judge in 1926, once again with Pendergast's backing. Despite being a Pendergast, he was known for being forthright and a master manager throughout his two four-year periods in office.

Due to the two-term tradition and the Pendergast machine's unwillingness to promote Truman to higher office, his political career seemed to be coming to an end in 1934. Pendergast presented the invitation to run for U.S. Senate to Truman, who promptly accepted, after many others turned down the machine's offer. With a majority of 40,000 votes in the primary, he seemed sure to win the election in the heavily Democratic state of Missouri. Truman was sworn in as the junior senator for Missouri by Vice President John Nance Garner in January 1935.

Even though Truman started off in the Senate cast as a pawn of the crooked Pendergast, his colleagues quickly warmed to him due to his amiability, honesty, and diligence in carrying out his responsibilities. Two landmark pieces of legislation, one regulating the aviation sector (the Civil Aeronautics Act of 1938) and the other overseeing the reorganisation of railroads (the Wheeler-Truman Transportation Act of 1940), were authored by him. He acquired national attention for spearheading an inquiry into fraud and waste in the U.S. military during his second term in the Senate, which he achieved after a difficult Democratic primary victory in 1940. The Truman Committee, formally known as the Special Committee Investigating National Defence, revealed manufacturing flaws and corruption while being careful not to disrupt the huge war preparation operation. Corporations, unions, and government organisations were often provided with draught reports outlining the committee's findings. This gave them the opportunity to address any abuses before official action was taken.

Truman, who was well-liked by both his fellow senators and the general public, was chosen to replace Henry A. Wallace as the Democratic nominee for vice president in 1944, succeeding Franklin Delano Roosevelt. On January 20, 1945, Truman took the oath of office as vice president, and the Roosevelt-Truman ticket received 53% of the vote, while its Republican opponents received 46%. But in the 82 days that he was in office, he had just two meetings with the president. Truman was unprepared for the weight of responsibility that was about to fall on him, and Roosevelt, who seemed unaware of his own illness, did nothing to apprise him of the administration's intentions and programmes.

# 42.

# LEON TROTSKY (RUSSIA)

Leon Trotsky was a prominent figure in the Russian October Revolution of 1917 and subsequently served as the Soviet Union's commissar of foreign affairs and war (1917–1924). He was born on November 7, 1879, in Yanovka, Ukraine, Russian Empire, and died on August 21, 1940, in Coyoacán, Mexico. Trotsky was a communist thinker and activist. But in the power struggle that followed Vladimir Ilich Lenin's death, Joseph Stalin came out on top, and Trotsky was banished from all positions of authority (1929). Until Stalin's agent assassinated him, he was the head of an anti-Stalinist movement overseas.

David Bronshtein, Trotsky's father, was a farmer from a Russified Jewish family who had lived in the steppe area as a colonist; Anna, Trotsky's mother, belonged to the educated middle class. Two younger siblings passed away when he was a baby, and he had an elder brother and sister. He spent eight years living with the family of a liberal thinker who was his mother's nephew before he was sent to school in Odessa when he was eight years old. He became enmeshed in an underground communist group and exposed to Marxism in 1896 when he relocated to Nikolayev to finish his education. He went to Odessa University for a semester before heading back to Nikolayev to assist with the clandestine South Russian Workers' Union.

While serving a four-and-a-half year sentence for revolutionary activities and exile in Siberia, Bronshtein wed his coconspirator Aleksandra Sokolovskaya and had two children. He was arrested in January 1898. In 1902, he jumped ship using a counterfeit passport that bore the name Trotsky, the revolutionary alias he had taken up. He eventually separated permanently from his wife, who stayed behind. After leaving Russia, Trotsky travelled to London to join a group of Russian Social-Democrats who were collaborating on the revolutionary publication Iskra ("The Spark") with Vladimir Ulyanov ("Lenin").

In July 1903, during the Second Congress of the Russian Social-Democratic Workers' Party, which was held in London and Brussels, Trotsky broke with Lenin and the Bolsheviks to support the Mensheviks, who argued for a more democratic form of socialism. Trotsky had met and married Natalya Sedova not long before this in Paris; they had two kids, Sergey and Lev, together.

When revolutionary unrest broke out in Russia in 1905, Trotsky went back to his home country. When the St. Petersburg Soviet (council) of Workers' Deputies organised a revolutionary strike movement and other forms of disobedience against the tsarist government, he became a key voice for them. Following this, Trotsky was arrested and tried in 1906. In "Results and Prospects," one of Trotsky's key publications, he lays forth his idea of perpetual revolution while he is detained.

Following his second banishment to Siberia in 1907, Trotsky managed to escape once again. After relocating to Vienna, he made a living as a war journalist covering the Balkan Wars (1912–13). Along with other Russian Social-Democrats, Trotsky denounced and refused to support the tsarist regime's war effort when World War I broke out. Before settling in Paris, he travelled to Switzerland. France and Spain banished him for his anti-war views. The Russian-language newspaper Novy Mir ("The New World") was edited by Nikolay Bukharin and he arrived in New York City in January 1917.

# 43.

# LYNDON B. JOHNSON (USA)

Johnson had the idea of "A Great Society" for all people, not just Americans. One of the most massive legislative programmes in U.S. history was passed during his first years in office. He continued the ever-increasing fight to contain Communist incursion in Vietnam while also ensuring collective security.

Johnson City, which his family had helped Johnson City, which his family had helped establish, was located in central Texas, and he was born there on August 27, 1908. Having grown up in rural Texas and worked his way through Southwest Texas State Teachers College (now called Texas State University–San Marcos), he gained empathy for others' plight as a teacher of Mexican American pupils.

His wife, the former Claudia "Lady Bird" Taylor, whom he wed in 1934, played a key role in his successful 1937 campaign for the House of Representatives on a New Deal platform.

He was awarded the Silver Star in the South Pacific during his short stint as a lieutenant commander in the Navy during World War II. In

1948, Johnson was elected to the Senate after six years in the House. He made history in 1953 as the Senate's youngest Minority Leader and then became the Majority Leader the year after the Democrats took power. A number of crucial Eisenhower legislation were passed because to his exceptional abilities.

Johnson was elected Vice President in 1960 while serving as John F. Kennedy's running partner. Johnson took the oath of office on November 22, 1963, the same day that Kennedy was shot dead.

First, he got a tax reduction and a new civil rights law passed, which were initiatives that President Kennedy had been pushing for before he died. "To build a great society, a place where the meaning of man's life matches the marvels of man's labour," he said, urging the nation. Johnson received 61% of the vote and the largest popular margin in U.S. history—over 15,000,000 votes—when he was elected president in 1964.

Aid to education, an assault on disease, Medicare, conservation, urban renewal, beautification, development of downtrodden areas, a massive battle against poverty, control and prevention of crime and delinquency, and the elimination of barriers to voting were all items on Johnson's agenda for Congress in January 1965. The suggestions put forward by Johnson were swiftly implemented by Congress, with occasional additions or revisions. With the Medicare expansion to the Social Security Act in 1965, millions of seniors finally had a safety net.

The United States conducted remarkable space expeditions under Johnson's presidency, a programme he had vigorously advocated for from the beginning. By successfully completing three lunar orbits in December 1968, Johnson praised the astronauts and said, "You've taken... all of us, all over the world, into a new era... "

But two major problems have been intensifying since 1965. The Nation was worried by riots and instability in black ghettos, even if new anti-discrimination and anti-poverty programmes had begun. Although President Johnson made steady efforts to combat segregation and promote law and order, no immediate resolution was achieved.

Vietnam also caused the second crisis. Fighting persisted despite Johnson's best attempts to halt Communist assault and reach a solution. At the tail end of March 1968, he curtailed bombing North Vietnam in order to start discussions, which stoked the growing war controversy. Concurrently, he shocked everyone by not running for re-election. This allowed him to focus entirely on the pursuit for peace, free from the distractions of politics.

He left office just as peace negotiations were beginning; he died of a heart attack at his ranch in Texas on January 22, 1973, thus he never got to see them through to a successful conclusion.

# 44.

# MUSTAFA KEMAL ATATÜRK (TURKEY)

Kemal Atatürk, known as "Kemal, Father of Turks" (born 1881 in Salonika, Greece; died November 10, 1938 in Istanbul, Turkey), was the first president of the Republic of Turkey (1923-38). He modernised the legal and educational institutions and supported European lifestyles, writing Turkish in the Latin script and giving individuals European names.

President Atatürk a 20th-century great, saved the Turkish remnant of the Ottoman Empire after World War I. He rallied his people against Greek invaders who wanted to impose the Allied will on the war-weary Turks and defeated British, French, and Italian soldiers. He built the present Republic of Turkey via these battles, and Turks still respect him. He revived Turkish pride and gave his people a feeling of success as they modernised. Over 20 years, Atatürk built a modern state that would become a democracy under his successors.

Mustafa Atatürk was born in Salonika, an Ottoman port, in 1881. His father, Ali Riza, was a lieutenant in a local militia unit during the Russo-Turkish War of 1877–78, suggesting he was somewhat Ottoman. Mustafa's mother, Zübeyde Hanım, was from an agricultural hamlet west of Salonika.

Ali Riza died when Mustafa was seven, but he shaped his personality. Ali Riza put his sword over his son's cradle upon his birth, committing him to the military. Ali Riza ensured his son's early education at a secular school, rather than the religious institution Zübeyde Hanım favoured. Ali Riza modernised his kid this way. Mustafa always owed his father this.

Zübeyde Hanım relocated to her step-brother's property near Salonika after Ali Riza's death. She sent Mustafa back to Salonika to attend a secular school for bureaucratic training out of concern that he would grow up ignorant. Mustafa loved his neighbourhood military cadet clothes. He decided to join the military. Mustafa took the military secondary school entrance test against his mother's objections.

The mathematics instructor gave Mustafa the moniker Kemal, meaning "The Perfect One," in high school. He entered Monastir's military academy in 1895. He gained many new acquaintances, notably Ali Fethi (Okyar), who helped him build the Turkish republic.

In March 1899, Mustafa Kemal attended the Istanbul War College after graduating from Monastir. His new buddy and classmate Ali Fuat (Cebesoy) exposed him to the city's independence and elegance, which he appreciated.

Political protest against Sultan Abdülhamid II's autocracy was strong in the War College. Mustafa Kemal was aloof until his third year, when he started a secret newspaper. He graduated as a second lieutenant in 1902 and placed in the top 10 of his class of over 450 pupils despite his actions being discovered. He subsequently attended the General Staff College and graduated as a captain in 1905, placing fifth out of 57. He was one of the empire's top young commanders.

# 45.

# LOUIS XIV (FRANCE)

The symbol of absolute monarchy of the classical age was Louis XIV, king of France (1643–1715), who ruled his country from his great palace at Versailles during one of its most brilliant periods. He increased France's eastern boundaries at the Habsburgs' cost in a series of conflicts between 1667 and 1697, and in the War of the Spanish Succession (1701–14), he fought a hostile European coalition to win the Spanish crown for his grandson.

The Louvre Museum, Paris, has Peter Paul Rubens' 1620/25 oil on canvas Anne of Austria. 85 × 37 cm.

Louis was born to Louis XIII and Anne of Austria. He succeeded his father May 14, 1643. According to kingdom law, he was the master and owner of 19 million subjects' bodies and possessions at four years and eight months. Despite being called "a visible divinity," he was a neglected youngster raised by slaves. He barely avoided drowning in a pond since no one was looking. Anne of Austria, who was negligent, instilled terror of "crimes committed against God."

Jules Cardinal Mazarin, Philippe de Champaigne portrait detail, Musée Condé, Chantilly, France.

Louis was nine years old when the nobility and Paris Parlement, a strong law court, revolted against the monarchy in 1648 out of hate of prime minister Jules Cardinal Mazarin. This started the Fronde, a protracted civil conflict in which Louis faced poverty, misery, terror, humiliation, cold, and hunger. These hardships influenced the young king's character, attitude, and philosophy. He would never forgive Paris, nobility, or commoners.

Mazarin defeated the rebels in 1653 and built an exceptional administrative system with Louis as his student. Young king inherited Mazarin's love of art, elegance, and presentation. Despite being of age, the king never challenged the cardinal's total control.

The 1635 France-Spain conflict was nearing its end. The conflict would give the Bourbons European dominion from the Habsburgs. A French monarch had to be a soldier, therefore Louis learned on the battlefield.

Princes of the time often struggled between love and duty, as Louis did in 1658. He fought with his love for Marie Mancini, Mazarin's niece, for two years. He ultimately gave in to politics and married Marie-Thérèse of Austria, daughter of King Philip IV of Spain, in 1660 to establish peace.

# 46.

# RICHARD NIXON (USA)

President Richard M. Nixon prioritised rapprochement. War abroad and urban unrest sowed deep divisions throughout the country. Nixon was able to improve ties with China and the Soviet Union and bring an end to American involvement in Vietnam during his presidency. However, he resigned as a result of the Watergate crisis, which further divided the nation.

His remarkable career, which began with early success and culminated in his 1968 victory, was notable for two reasons: first, he had been unsuccessful in his bids for president in 1960 and for governor of California in 1962.

Nixon began his legal career after achieving stellar academic results at Whittier College and Duke University Law School. Nixon was born in California in 1913. Patricia (Tricia) and Julie were his children from his marriage to Patricia Ryan in 1940. Nixon oversaw the Pacific Fleet as a lieutenant commander during WWII.

When he left the military, he won reelection to represent his California district in Congress. He was elected to the Senate in 1950.

Eisenhower chose Nixon, who was 39 years old at the time, to be his running partner two years down the road.

During Eisenhower's presidency, Nixon was heavily involved in many executive functions as vice president. He was John F. Kennedy's narrowly defeated opponent in the 1960 acclamation run for president. After reclaiming his party's candidature in 1968, he went on to dethrone Hubert H. Humphrey, the vice president, and George C. Wallace, a third-party contender.

While in government, he oversaw revenue sharing, repealed the draught, passed new anti-crime legislation, and established a comprehensive environmental programme. He kept his word and selected conservative intellectuals to the Supreme Court. In 1969, during his first term in office, American astronauts accomplished a historic feat—the first lunar landing.

In his fight for global peace and security, he accomplished some of his most celebrated feats. He eased tensions with China and the USSR during 1972 travels to Moscow and Beijing. A pact to restrict strategic nuclear weapons was the result of his summit discussions with Russian leader Leonid I. Brezhnev. He declared an end to U.S. engagement in Indochina in January 1973 after a deal was struck with North Vietnam. Israel and its adversaries, Egypt and Syria, reached disengagement agreements in 1974 via Henry Kissinger, his secretary of state.

Nixon won reelection in 1972 by a historically large margin against Democratic nominee George McGovern.

The so-called "Watergate" scandal, which began with a 1972 campaign break-in at the Democratic National Committee's headquarters, quickly engulfed his government. Committee to Re-elect the President officers were identified as the perpetrators of the break-in. Many government officials stepped down after being accused of trying to cover up the situation or were eventually found guilty of related crimes. The courts coerced Nixon into turning over audio recordings that proved he had attempted to derail the probe, despite his denials of any personal participation.

The resignation of Vice President Spiro T. Agnew in 1973 was caused by unconnected incidents in Maryland. Senate Minority Leader Gerald R. Ford was nominated by Nixon and confirmed by Congress to the position of vice president.

Nixon, who seemed to be heading straight towards impeachment, announced his resignation on August 8, 1974, with the intention of starting "that process of healing which is so desperately needed in America" the following day.

Nixon was hailed as an older statesman in his latter years. Prior to his death on April 22, 1994, he had written a plethora of books spanning his tenure in public office and his thoughts on international affairs.

# 47.

# FIDEL CASTRO (CUBA)

The political leader of Cuba from 1959 to 2008, Fidel Castro was born August 13, 1926, in Birán, Cuba, and died November 25, 2016, Cuba. Cuba became the first communist state in the Western Hemisphere under Castro's leadership. For the Latin American communist revolution, Castro became a symbol. Before beginning his lengthy career as president of the Council of State and the Council of Ministers, he held the position of premier until 1976. Due to health issues, he temporarily ceded power in July 2006, and he officially stepped down as president in February 2008.

Southeastern Cuba is where Castro was born. Ángel Castro y Argiz, who came to the United States from Spain as an immigrant, was a successful sugarcane grower in an area that had been controlled by the United Fruit Company for a long time. In the midst of his marriage to his first wife, Ángel Castro started an affair with Lina Ruz González, a servant, whom he would eventually wed. Fidel was one of seven children born to this union, and Raúl was another. Raúl went on to become Fidel's main ally in Cuban politics.

Before attending the Catholic high school Belén in Havana, where he excelled as a sportsman, Fidel Castro attended Roman Catholic boarding schools in Santiago de Cuba. His athletic prowess in baseball, basketball, table tennis and track and field (particularly the high jump and medium distance running) earned him the title of Havana's finest schoolboy athlete in 1943–1944. He enrolled at the University of Havana's School of Law in 1945, a time when violent gangs pursued a variety of objectives, including love fulfilment, political power, and professional advancement. In 1947, Castro participated in a failed plot by Cubans and Dominican exiles to invade the Dominican Republic and depose General Rafael Trujillo; this was his primary political involvement while at university. He then became involved in the April 1948 urban riots in Bogotá, Colombia.

Castro joined the reformist Ortodoxos faction of the Cuban People's Party and went on to practise law after graduating in 1950. He was nominated to represent a Havana district in the upcoming June 1952 House of Representatives elections. But the elections were cancelled and the administration of Pres. Carlos Prío Socarrás was deposed in March of that year by the previous president of Cuba, Gen. Fulgencio Batista.

Castro started to create a rebel group in 1953 when legal measures failed to depose Batista's new regime. He attempted to incite a popular revolt by leading 160 men in a suicide assault on the Moncada military barracks in Santiago de Cuba on July 26, 1953. Along with the capture of Castro, the majority of the guys were slain. His passionate defence at trial resulted in a 15-year jail term handed down by the state. After being granted political amnesty in 1955, he and his brother Raúl travelled to Mexico to carry on their resistance against the Batista government. The 26th of July Movement was Fidel Castro's revolutionary organisation for Cuban exiles.

The yacht Granma landed Castro and an armed detachment of eighty-one men on Cuba's eastern coast on December 2, 1956. Except for Fidel and Raúl Castro, Ernesto ("Che") Guevara, and nine others, who withdrew into the Sierra Maestra to engage in guerilla warfare against the Batista troops, everyone else was either murdered or captured. The demoralised and poorly commanded military forces of the Batista administration were repeatedly defeated by Fidel Castro's troops, who were aided by an increasing number of revolutionary volunteers throughout the island. Following a decline in domestic political support and a string of military losses, Batista departed the nation on January 1, 1959, thanks in large part to Castro's persuasive rhetoric. The 30,000-man professional army of the Cuban government was vanquished by Castro's 800 guerillas.

# 48.

# SALADIN (AYYUBID SULTANATE)

He was the Muslim Sultan of Egypt and Syria (r. 1174-1193) who stunned the western world by defeating an army of Christian Crusader kingdoms at the Battle of Hattin and then taking Jerusalem in 1187. Saladin was born in 1137 and died in 1193. On the other hand, Saladin was able to effectively resist the Third Crusade (1187-1192) and almost completely wipe out the Latin East powers that were located in the Levant.

By using a formidable combination of military might, diplomatic manoeuvres, and the prospect of holy war, Saladin was able to fulfil his goal of uniting the Muslim Near East, which stretched from Egypt to Arabia. "Saladin's skills in warfare and politics, as well as his personal qualities of generosity and chivalry, resulted in him being eulogised by both Christian and Muslim writers so that he has become one of the most famous figures of the Middle Ages and the subject of countless literary works ever since his death in his favourite gardens of Damascus in 1193."

Saladin, whose full name was al-Malik al-Nasir Salah al-Dunya wa'l-Din Abu'l Muzaffar Yusuf Ibn Ayyub Ibn Shadi al-Kurdi, was born in the year 1137 in the fortress of Takrit, which is located to the north of Baghdad. His father, Ayub, was a Kurdish mercenary who had been banished from his homeland. In the course of his career in the military, Saladin would earn a reputation for being a talented polo player and a skillful horseman. He would climb through the ranks of the military. During the war that his uncle Shirkuh led to the conquest of Egypt in 1169, he accompanied him. After that, Saladin succeeded his relative as governor of Egypt for Nur ad-Din, who was also an independent governor of Aleppo and Edessa during the reign of 1146-1174. Nur ad-Din is often further referred to as Nur al-Din. When it comes to describing the youthful Saladin, the historian J. Phillips provides the following short description:

When Nur ad-Din passed away in May of 1174, his alliance of Muslim kingdoms eventually disintegrated, and his successors engaged in a struggle for dominance. With the assertion that he was the rightful successor, Saladin seized control of Egypt for himself.

# 49.

# DENG XIAOPING (CHINA)

Born on August 22, 1904, in Guang'an, Sichuan province, China, Deng Xiaoping was a communist leader and the most influential person in the People's Republic of China from the late 1970s until his death in 1997. He passed away on February 19, 1997, in Beijing. In an effort to modernise China's economy, he rejected many traditional communist principles and instead advocated for free-enterprise principles.

Deng, whose father was a landowner, attended university in France (1920–24) and the Soviet Union (1925–26), where he became politically involved. He went back to China and rose through the ranks to become a top military and political organiser in Mao Zedong's independent communist enclave in southern China, the Jiangxi Soviet, which he had founded in 1931. Deng took part in the Chinese communists' long and gruelling march (1934–1935) to a new stronghold in Shaanxi province, northwest China, after the communists were ousted in 1934 by Nationalist troops led by Chiang Kai-shek. He was a political officer and commissar for a section of the Eighth Route Army of the communists from 1937 until 1945. After that, he became a secretary of the CCP. During the Chinese Civil War (1947–49), Deng was also the head commissar of the communist Second Field Army. He rose through the ranks to become the party chief of southern China after the communist seizure of the country in 1949. He was appointed vice premier in 1952 after being called to Beijing. He rose swiftly through the ranks and was named CCP general secretary in 1954 and a member of the governing Political Bureau in 1955.

Deng began to play a significant role in formulating internal and international policy in the mid-1950s. He had strong alliances with pragmatic leaders like Liu Shaoqi, who advocated for materialism and the cultivation of top technical and managerial talent as means to China's economic success. With Deng's focus on individual self-interest at odds with Mao's emphasis on egalitarianism and revolutionary zeal, the two leaders' ideologies became more divisive.

Radical Maoists opposed Deng during the Cultural Revolution (1966–1976). After losing all of his high-ranking party and government positions between 1967 and 1969, he vanished from public consciousness. Nevertheless, Deng was re-instated and promoted to the position of deputy premier in 1973, due to Premier Zhou Enlai's patronage. In 1975, he assumed the roles of vice-chairman of the party's Central Committee, member of its Politburo, and head of the general staff. He was generally believed to be Zhou's potential successor after serving as de facto head of state in the months leading up to Zhou's death. Nevertheless, Deng was once again removed from leadership after Zhou's demise in January 1976 by the Gang of Four, the Cultural Revolution's pro-Mao extreme elite. Deng was rehabilitated with the approval of Hua Guofeng, Mao's designated heir to China's leadership, after Mao's death in September 1976 & the Gang of Four's subsequent fall from power.

# 50.

# QUEEN VICTORIA (UK)

Victoria was queen of the United Kingdom of Great Britain and Ireland (1837–1901) and empress of India (1876–1901). The Victorian Age was named after the final Hanover House member. The British monarchy became ceremonial under her. Her nine children with Prince Consort Albert of Saxe-Coburg-Gotha gave rise to numerous European royal families.

Victoria heard about her destiny as a princess in a history class at age 10. Nearly four decades later, Victoria's governess recounted that the future queen said, "I will be good." The seriousness and egotism of Victoria's age defined her. The queen opposed Victorian ideals and advancements. Victoria ruled a culture that idealised motherhood and the family, even though she disliked pregnancy and delivery, infants, and children. She didn't care about social concerns, although Britain was reforming in the 19th century. She fought technological progress while mechanical and technological advances transformed European culture.

Most importantly, Victoria was a queen intent to maintain political authority, but she accidentally transformed the sovereign's function from political to ceremonial, preserving the British monarchy. The political significance of the crown and the throne's permanency were unclear when Victoria became queen. When she died and her son Edward VII moved from Marlborough House to Buckingham Palace, the alteration was social rather than political; the monarchy would survive. Her rule was measured by it.

After Princess Charlotte, daughter of the prince regent (later George IV), died in 1817, George III's 15 children had no legal descendants. To ensure succession, his sons Clarence, Kent, and Cambridge married in 1818. Edward, duke of Kent, George III's fourth son, won the contest to father the next British king. He named his only kid Alexandrina Victoria. Victoria became third in the line of succession to the throne after the duke of York (died 1827) and the duke of Clarence (later William IV), whose children died in infancy.

Victoria "was brought up very simply," mostly at Kensington Palace, where her closest friends were her half sister, Féodore, and her governess, Louise (later the Baroness) Lehzen, from Coburg. An significant father figure to the orphaned princess was her uncle Leopold, her mother's brother, who resided at Claremont, near Esher, Surrey, until he became king of Belgium in 1831.

Sir John Conroy, the duchess of Kent's counsellor, made Victoria's upbringing worse. Conroy planned to rule the future queen of Britain while controlling the docile duchess. After Conroy convinced her that the royal dukes, “the wicked uncles,” threatened her daughter, the duchess raised Victoria using “the Kensington system,” which secluded her from her peers and her father's relatives. So Conroy wanted to make the princess reliant on and readily led by him.

# 51.

# JAWAHARLAL NEHRU (INDIA)

A rich Kashmiri Pandit lawyer called Motilal Nehru and his wife Swaruprani Thussu had their first son, Jawaharlal, on November 14, 1889. In the Northwest Provinces of British India (now Uttar Pradesh), the family resided in Allahabad. Two sisters with distinguished occupations joined Little Nehru.

Nehru was taught at home by governesses and later private tutors. Science was his forte, whereas religion was his least interest. Nehru became an Indian patriot early in life and was elated by Japan's victory over Russia in the Russo-Japanese War (1905). This inspired him to dream "of Indian freedom and Asiatic freedom from the thraldom of Europe."

Nehru studied at Winston Churchill's alma school, Harrow School, in England aged 16. In 1910, he earned an honours degree in botany, chemistry, and geology from Trinity College, Cambridge, two years after entering in 1907. Besides Keynesian economics, the young Indian patriot studied history, literature, and politics in university.

His father persuaded Nehru to study law at the Inner Temple in London in October 1910. Following his legal admission in 1912, Jawaharlal Nehru decided to sit the Indian Civil Service exam & utilise his degree to combat British colonial laws and practises.

By the time he returned to India, he had been exposed to socialist ideals, which were popular among British intellectuals. Nehru established socialism as a basis of contemporary India.

at August 1912, Jawaharlal Nehru returned to India and practised law half-heartedly at the Allahabad High Court. Young Nehru found law stifling and "insipid."

He was more impressed by the 1912 Indian National Congress (INC) annual session, but its elitism disappointed him. Nehru joined Gandhi's 1913 campaign, starting a decades-long partnership. His focus shifted from law to politics during the following three years.

Most upper-class Indians backed the Allies throughout WWI (1914-18) and loved seeing Britain humiliated. Nehru was torn but grudgingly supported the Allies, favouring France over Britain.

World War I saw almost 1 million Indian and Nepalese troops fight for the Allies, 62,000 of them perished. Many Indian nationalists anticipated favours from Britain after the war in exchange for their loyalty, but many were severely disappointed.

# 52.

# VLADIMIR PUTIN (RUSSIA)

Vladimir Putin (born October 7, 1952, Leningrad, Russia, U.S.S.R. [now St. Petersburg, Russia]) is a Russian intelligence officer and politician who served as president (1999–2008 and 2012–) and prime minister (1999 and 2008–12).

Putin studied law at Leningrad State University under Anatoly Sobchak, a perestroika reformist. Putin was a KGB foreign intelligence officer for 15 years, six of them in Dresden, East Germany. He resigned from the KGB as a lieutenant colonel in 1990 and returned to Russia to become Leningrad State University's prorector for foreign relations. Putin then advised St. Petersburg's first democratically elected mayor, Sobchak. He became first deputy mayor in 1994 after winning Sobchak's trust and being adept at getting things done.

Putin went to Moscow in 1996 to work as Pavel Borodin's deputy on the presidential staff. Putin rose in administration and became close to Leningrader Anatoly Chubais. Putin became secretary of the Security

Council when Boris Yeltsin appointed him head of the Federal Security Service (FSB), the KGB's domestic replacement, in July 1998. Putin became prime minister in 1999 as Yeltsin was looking for a successor.

Putin's popular favour rose as he led a well-organized military campaign against Chechen separatists despite his anonymity. After years of Yeltsin's antics, the Russian people admired Putin's composure. Putin's backing of Unity assured its victory in the December legislative elections.

Yeltsin abruptly resigned and declared Putin interim president on December 31, 1999. Austere and restrained Putin comfortably won the March 2000 elections with 53% of the vote, promising to restore a weaker Russia. He fought corruption and established a highly regulated market economy as president.

Putin immediately reorganised Russia's 89 provinces and republics into seven federal districts led by presidential appointees. Regional governors lost their privilege to sit in the Federation Council, Russia's upper legislature. Putin closed multiple media outlets and began criminal procedures against several "oligarchs" to weaken their authority. In 2002, Putin proclaimed the military war in Chechnya completed, although losses remained high due to rebels' terrorist assaults in Moscow and guerrilla attacks on Russian forces from the region's mountains.

Putin fiercely opposed George W. Bush's 2001 abandonment of the 1972 Anti-Ballistic Missile Treaty. After the 2001 September 11 attacks, Putin offered Russia's airspace for humanitarian supplies and search-and-rescue missions in the U.S.-led war against terrorists and their allies. In 2002–03, Putin, Schröder, and Chirac opposed U.S. and British attempts to overthrow Saddam Hussein's regime in Iraq.

In March 2004, Putin was handily reelected thanks to a growing economy following the 1990s recession. In December 2007, Putin's United Russia party secured a landslide majority in parliament. International observers and the Communist Party of Russia questioned the elections' impartiality, but the results confirmed Putin's control. Putin appointed Dmitry Medvedev as his successor in 2008 due to a constitutional need.

# 53.

# HENRY VIII (UK)

Henry VIII was born in Greenwich on 28 June 1491, the second son of Henry VII and Elizabeth of York. After his older brother Prince Arthur died in 1502, he ascended in 1509.

He was smart and athletic as a kid. A contemporary characterised him as 'he speaks fluent French, Latin, and Spanish; is exceedingly pious; heard three masses everyday while hunting... He loves hunting and always keeps eight or 10 horses. He likes tennis.

Henry was a generous supporter of the arts and wrote books and music.

His musical skills included composition and instrument playing. However, Greensleeves, the famous music, is unlikely to be his.

The Pope named Henry 'Defender of the Faith' in 1521 after his best-selling book, which had 20 English and European editions, attacked Martin Luther and supported the Roman Catholic church.

When he succeeded his father, Henry VIII inherited a stable kingdom with a surplus of money. Parliament had not been called for supplies in five years. Henry's various interests and lack of political experience boosted Thomas Wolsey's authority as Lord Chancellor in 1515.

Wolsey built Hampton Court Palace, which was larger than the king's, making him one of the most influential ministers in British history. Wolsey actively used the Council's judicial authority in the Star Chamber and his own Chancery.

Cardinal Wolsey was granted papal legate powers in 1515 to bypass the Archbishop of Canterbury and 'govern' the Church in England.

Henry concentrated his foreign strategy on Western Europe, a fluctuating coalition of the monarchs of Spain and France and the Holy Roman Emperor. Henry's wife Katherine was Ferdinand of Aragon's daughter, his sister Mary married Louis IX of France in 1514, and Katherine's nephew Charles V was the Holy Roman Emperor Charles V.

Henry lavished money on demonstrations and tournaments in the Field of the Cloth of Gold during his fruitless Anglo-Spanish operations against France, which ended in peace in 1520.

Henry expanded the fleet from 5 to 53 ships, including the Mary Rose; its remnants are at the Portsmouth Naval Museum.

The succession and the Protestant Reformation, which created the Church of England, dominated Henry's second half.

Henry married Catherine of Aragon, his brother's widow, in 1509. Catherine had one daughter, Princess Mary, born in 1516. In the late 1520s, Henry's wife was in her 40s and he wanted a son.

Henry was the second Tudor king after the 1485 conquest. England had no queen, and the monarchy was too unstable to risk disputed succession or foreign power dominance by marrying a woman.

Anyway, Henry fell in love with Anne Boleyn, the sister of one of his numerous mistresses, and sought to get the Pope to dissolve his marriage on the grounds that it was never lawful.

The royals have divorced before: Louis IX in 1499 and James IV's widow Margaret (Henry's sister) in 1528. Henry was permitted to marry his brother's widow by a previous Pope in 1509.

Wolsey failed to get the Pope's consent to settle Henry's lawsuit in England in May 1529. Henry and his counsellors failed; Wolsey was fired, jailed, and died before trial.

After failing to persuade the pope for the divorce, Wolsey's successor Thomas Cromwell (Henry's principal counsel from 1532 forward) went to Parliament, which used its powers and anti-clerical stance (encouraged by Wolsey's excesses) to determine the matter.

Acts reduced papal rule in England and sparked the English Reformation.

In 1532, an Act against Annates, postponed at 'the king's discretion', warned the Pope that church income were threatened.

Cranmer was elevated to Archbishop of Canterbury in 1532 and proclaimed Henry's marriage unlawful in May 1533 when the Pope confirmed his appointment. Anne Boleyn was crowned queen a week later.

After the Pope excommunicated Henry, Parliament passed laws approving his separation with the Roman Catholic Church. The Act in restraint of appeals prohibited appeals to Rome because England was an empire ruled by one supreme head and monarch with 'full and whole' power and thus Rome's verdicts and excommunications were invalid.

Following the Act of Submission of the Clergy, Act of Succession, and Act of Supremacy (1534), the king became 'the single ultimate head of the Church of England termed Anglicana Ecclesia'.

The break between the monarch and the Pope caused clergy, office-holders, and others to select sides, including Sir Thomas More, who was beheaded for treason in 1535.

English Protestant Reformation also led to the dissolution and sale of monastery estates and holdings. Wolsey disbanded several tiny monastic groups in 1518 to fund his new foundations (Oxford and Ipswich colleges).

In 1535-6, 200 lesser monasteries were dissolved by legislation, followed by the remaining major houses in 1538-40; Crown income quadrupled for a few years.

Henry's second marriage led to dreams of a son. Boleyn had another daughter, Princess Elizabeth, but no son. Henry executed Anne in 1536 on spurious treason accusations concocted by Thomas Cromwell and presided over by her uncle, the Duke of Norfolk. Her successor, Henry's third wife Jane Seymour, gave birth to Edward VI in 1537. In 1537, Jane died in childbed 12 days after delivery.

Cromwell felt uneasy despite his success in bringing about the royal divorce and English Reformation. The 1536 Pilgrimage of Grace revolt demanded Cromwell's departure, but Henry's fourth, unsuccessful, and short-lived marriage to Anne of Cleves brought him down. Three months after becoming Earl of Essex in 1540, he was seized and killed.

Henry married Katherine Howard (executed for adultery in 1542) and Catherine Parr (who survived Henry to die in 1548).

They had no children. Henry educated his single son, Edward, by Protestants rather than Catholics to strengthen his anti-papal reformation and dynasty.

In Henry's last seven years, no dominant minister arose after Cromwell's execution. Henry, overweight, irritable, and sick, returned to France.

The French campaign collapsed after capturing only Boulogne with 40,000 soldiers. Even though more than half the monastery holdings had been sold, forced loans and currency devaluation were used to pay for the war, raising inflation. Edward succeeded Henry as king after his death in London on 28 January 1547.

Henry VIII's Church-State reforms removed the pope and centralised the clergy, strengthening the Crown and gaining the monasteries' riches, according to some.

However, Henry's reformation caused deadly Protestant-Roman Catholic divisions throughout the country. Wartime spending by the monks had strengthened the counties' nobility and other households, encouraging ambitious Tudor court factions.

Parliament's role in religious and dynastic transitions was well-established. Despite his concern over establishing his dynasty and religious upheaval, Henry's six marriages had produced one sickly son and an insecure succession with two princesses (Mary and Elizabeth), both of whom had been declared illegitimate and never had children.

# 54.

# CHE GUEVARA (ARGENTINA)

Che Guevara was a revolutionary leader from Cuba who was born in Argentina and became a hero to the left. An picture of him taken by photographer Alberto Korda became a defining symbol of the twentieth century.

Che Guevara, whose real name is Ernesto Guevara de la Serna, was born into a middle-class family in Rosario, Argentina on June 14, 1928. While attending medical school in Buenos Aires, he extensively toured across South and Central America. He believed that armed revolution was the only way to solve the issues in Central and South America due to his interest on Marxism and the tremendous poverty and tyranny he saw.

He visited Mexico in 1954 and met Fidel Castro, the revolutionary leader of Cuba, the following year. When Castro's "26th July Movement" guerilla fight against Fulgencio Batista, Cuba's ruler, broke out, Guevara was an integral part of it.

In 1959, Castro toppled Batista and assumed control of Cuba. After serving as minister of industry from 1959 to 1961, Guevara became head of Cuba's National Bank. He represented Cuba on a global scale while serving in this capacity. Back home, he put his ideas for nationalising industries and redistributing land into action.

He led Castro's government towards Soviet alignment and was a staunch opponent of the US. Due to American trade restrictions and measures that failed, the Cuban economy collapsed. A rift sprang up between Guevara and the other Cuban leaders during this challenging period. After Guevara departed Cuba, he wanted to take the revolution to other underdeveloped countries, which Castro stated in 1965.

In an effort to educate rebel groups in guerilla tactics, Guevara subsequently spent a number of months in Africa, focusing on the Congo. After his attempts were unsuccessful, he went back to Cuba in 1966 undercover. He went to Bolivia from Cuba to take charge of the rebels fighting against René Barrientos Ortuño's administration. Guevara and his surviving militants were arrested by the Bolivian army with the help of the US. His remains was buried in an undisclosed place after his execution on October 9, 1967, in the Bolivian town of La Higuera. He was reinterred in Cuba when his body was found, excavated, and returned there in 1997.

# 55.

# WILLIAM THE CONQUEROR (UK)

When William the Conqueror, also known as William, Duke of Normandy, fought and killed his adversary Harold Godwinson at the Battle of Hastings in 1066, he had successfully led the Norman Conquest of England. William the Conqueror lived approximately from 1027 to 1087. In 1066, on Christmas Day, he was crowned King William I of England, and after five years of gruelling warfare against rebels and invaders, he finally secured his new country via his reign.

William's policy of land redistribution among the Norman aristocracy insured that over the course of the subsequent centuries, the histories of England and France would be inextricably linked. This was accomplished while William continued to rule over Normandy. William, who was a skilled negotiator, a great military leader, and a cruel ruler, passed away in Caen, Normandy, in the year 1087 due to natural causes. His mausoleum is still located there.

Around the year 1027, William was born at Falaise, which is located in Normandy. William the Bastard is a nickname that is often used to refer to him since he was the son of Duke Robert I of Normandy (1028-1035) who was not legitimately born. Herleve of Falaise was William's mother. She was the daughter of a rich merchant in Rouen who also served as a chamberlain to the ducal court. William was named after her. Due to the fact that they were born to the same mother, William's half-brothers were Odo of Bayeux, who was the bishop of that city and would later become the Earl of Kent, and Robert, who would later become the Count of Mortain. In the year 1053, or 1050 according to some historians, William tied the knot with Mathilda, who passed away in the year 1083. Mathilda was the daughter of the Count of Flanders and the niece of Henry I of France, who ruled from 1031 to 1060. This marriage served to neatly consolidate the existing diplomatic links between the three territories. They would have four boys and four (or five) girls if they were to have children together.

# 56.

# EMPEROR CONSTANTINE (ROMAN EMPIRE)

Constantine, Roman Emperor (c. 280–337 A.D.), was a major figure in antiquity. By becoming Christianity the state religion of the enormous Roman Empire, he legitimised a faith that had previously been considered heretical. Constantine the Great finalised Christian teaching at the Council of Nicea. And when he founded Constantinople (after known as Byzantium), the capital of the Byzantine Empire, he put in motion events that would divide the Christian church, bring an end to the empire, and shape European history for the next thousand years.

Naissus, in the province of Moesia Superior, which is now part of Serbia, is the place where Flavius Valerius Constantinus was born. A barmaid called Helena and a military commander named Constantius were Constantine's parents. The emperor Constantius I would be his father, and Constantine's mother, Helena, who was said to have recovered a piece of Jesus' cross, would be canonised as a saint.

Theodora, daughter of Emperor Maximian, met Constantius's need for a pedigree bride when he became governor of Dalmatia. In Nicomedia, Constantine and Helena were escorted to Diocletian, the ruler of the East.

Constantine was acclaimed Caesar by his father's armies after his death on July 25, 306 A.D. Many others had also staked a claim. The Tetrarchy, instituted by Emperor Diocletian in 285, saw two senior emperors and two non-hereditary juniors govern each quadrant of the Roman Empire. A senior emperor, Constantius had served. Maximian and his son Maxentius, who had seized power in Italy and controlled Sardinia, Corsica, and Africa, were Constantine's most formidable opponents for the throne.

Constantine assembled a Germanic and Celtish army in Britain; according to the Byzantine historian Zosimus, there were 90,000 foot men and 8,000 horse. In all, Maxentius mustered 180,000 foot troops and 18,000 riders in his army.

Meeting Maxentius at the Milvian Bridge, Constantine marched on Rome on October 28, 312. According to legend, Constantine vowed to devote himself fully to Christianity in the event that he were to overcome tremendous obstacles and see the words in hoc signo vinces ("in this sign you will conquer") written on a cross. (Constantine fought against being baptised all the way to his deathbed.) After triumphing while bearing a cross, Constantine issued the Edict of Milan, legalising Christianity throughout the Empire, the next year.

Constantine and his brother-in-law Licinius divided the empire after Maxentius' defeat. East was governed by Licinius and West by Constantine. After ten years of tense truces, the two continued to be bitter enemies until their hatred reached a boiling point in the 324 Battle of Chrysopolis. After defeating Licinius, Constantine became Rome's only emperor.

Constantine built Constantinople atop the ruins of Byzantium, the stronghold of Licinius, as a symbol of his triumph. With his expansion plans, Alexander fortified the city and added many temples as well as a massive hippodrome for chariot racing. A second Senate was also created by him. Following the fall of Rome, Constantinople assumed the role of imperial seat in practise.

# 57.

# BARACK OBAMA (USA)

As the first African American to serve as president, Barack Obama made history in 2008. It was always the intention of the Constitution's authors that our nation's leadership would be open to all citizens, regardless of their financial status or familial ties. Being influenced by the biases of their day (many of whom had slaves), the majority of them would not have anticipated a president of African American descent. President Barack Obama was born to Stanley Ann Dunham and Barack Sr., an economist from Kenya, on August 4, 1961, in Hawaii. The couple met as students there. They eventually got a divorce, and Barack's mom remarried an Indonesian guy. He spent his early years there. He lived with his maternal grandparents in Honolulu before returning to Punahou School on a scholarship before fifth grade.

During his teenage years, Obama navigated the challenges of coming into his own, as detailed in his book Dreams from My Father (1995). He spent his first two years of college in Los Angeles's Occidental College before transferring to Columbia University to major in international affairs and politics. After finishing college in 1983, Obama worked in the Big Apple before settling into a role as a community organiser on Chicago's South Side. There, he collaborated with local churches to alleviate housing shortages and establish job-training programmes for residents who had lost their jobs due to the closing of nearby steel mills. After enrolling at Harvard Law School in 1988, he became famous throughout the country when he became the first African American to serve as president of the law review. After making his way back to Chicago, he became a partner at a boutique civil rights company.

A fellow Harvard Law School alumna, Michelle Robinson was Obama's spouse in 1992. Malia was born in 1998 and Sasha in 2001; the two of them are daughters. Before being elected to the United States Senate in 2004, Obama served as a senator for Illinois from 1996 to 2004. His keynote speech that summer at the Democratic National Convention was well praised. While some commentators predicted his presidency would materialise soon, the majority did not. But in 2008, he prevailed with 365 electoral votes to 173 for Arizona Senator John McCain.

The economic collapse, the wars in Afghanistan and Iraq, and the persistent threat of terrorism were just a few of the obstacles that Obama encountered as the new president. Obama, who aimed to restore America's global standing and implement historic government spending to boost the economy, was inaugurated before an estimated audience of 1.8 million people. Three measures bearing his signature were passed during his first term: one to restructure the nation's financial institutions; another to increase the availability and affordability of health care; and a third to boost the economy. A fair pay act for women, legislation to regulate the banking sector, and consumer protection were all priorities for Obama. Having accepted the Nobel Peace Prize in 2009, Obama joined a select group of presidents who have done so.

With 332 electoral votes against Romney's 206, he easily won reelection in 2012. For international policy, the Middle East continued to be an important obstacle. Obama presided over bin Laden's assassination, but in the midst of Syria's civil war, a new self-proclaimed Islamic State emerged and started instigating terrorist acts. Obama hoped that a nuclear arms pact would help contain an aggressive Iran. In addition, 195 countries' climate change accord to cut emissions of greenhouse gases and delay the onset of global warming was endorsed by the Obama administration.

During his last year in office, Obama gave speeches at two events that deeply touched him: the National Museum of African American History and Culture's dedication and the 50th anniversary of the civil rights march from Selma to Montgomery. During his speech in Selma, he acknowledged that the union was far from perfect but that they were drawn closer. As he addressed the crowd at the Washington museum opening, he said, "And that's why we celebrate, mindful that our work is not yet done."

# 58.

# GOLDA MEIR (ISRAEL)

Israeli politician Golda Meir was born May 3, 1898, in Kiev, Ukraine, and died December 8, 1978, in Jerusalem. She was instrumental in the establishment of the State of Israel in 1948 and was its fourth prime minister from 1969 to 1974. This position has never before been held by a woman. Goldie Mabovitch was born into a Jewish family that moved to Milwaukee, Wisconsin in 1906.

She got involved with the Milwaukee Labour Zionist Party after attending what is now the University of Wisconsin–Milwaukee, Milwaukee Normal School. Morris Myerson and her emigrated to Palestine in 1921, when they became members of the Merδavya kibbutz. From 1928 to 1932, she served as secretary of the Histadrut's Women's Labour Council, and from 1934 until World War II, she was a member of the organization's executive committee. She also became the kibbutz's delegate to the General Federation of Labour. While negotiating to the British required authorities, she became a powerful advocate for the Zionist cause throughout the war. Goldie Myerson temporarily succeeded Moshe Sharett as head of the Jewish Agency's Political Department in 1946 after he was detained by the British. Myerson fought for the release of her colleagues and the numerous Jewish war refugees who had broken British immigration laws by settling in Palestine. After he was released, Sharett assumed diplomatic responsibilities and formally succeeded to his post. She made an effort to convince King ʿAbdullāh I of Jordan not to join the Arab invasion of Israel.

In the same year that she was appointed minister to Moscow, Goldie Myerson signed Israel's independence proclamation on May 14, 1948. From 1949 to 1974, she was a member of Israel's parliament, the Knesset. She strongly advocated for the idea of unfettered Jewish immigration to Israel and oversaw massive housing and road development projects during her tenure as minister of labour (1949–1956). After being named Golda Meir in Hebraic, she was appointed foreign minister in 1956. She advocated for Israel's goal of aiding the newly formed African governments in an effort to win over reluctant countries' diplomats. She was prime minister Levi Eshkol's ally in party disputes and became secretary-general of the Mapai Party soon after her January 1966 retirement from the Foreign Ministry. She was instrumental in uniting Mapai with two other dissident groups to form the Israel Labour Party after Israel's triumph in the Six-Day War (June 1967) over Jordan, Syria, and Egypt.

Meir, the moderate candidate, succeeded Eshkol as prime minister after his death on February 26, 1969. She oversaw the continuation of the June 1967 coalition government. Meir used diplomatic channels to push for a Middle East peace accord. She met with Pope Paul VI in the Vatican (1973) and Nicolae Ceaușescu in Romania (1972), among other places she visited. Willy Brandt, chancellor of West Germany, was also hosted by Meir's cabinet in 1973.

When the Yom Kippur conflict broke out in October 1973, the fourth Arab-Israeli conflict, her attempts to negotiate a settlement with the Arab nations came to a standstill. Meir created a new coalition government with tremendous difficulty in March 1974 and resigned her seat as prime minister on April 10, startled by Israel's lack of war preparation. Until a new administration was established in June, she continued to hold power as head of a caretaker government. Even though she retired after it, she was still a major player in politics. It was discovered that she had suffered from leukaemia for twelve years before she passed away. In 1975, her autobiography, The Story of My Life, was released.

# 59.

# TONY BLAIR (UK)

Edinburgh, Scotland was the birthplace of Tony Blair in 1953. He took a year off before going to Oxford to study law; he eventually became a lawyer after graduation.

After becoming a member of the Labour Party in 1975, he mounted a successful campaign for the safe seat of Sedgefield in 1983. By1983, Gordon Brown had also been elected, and the two had become close friends.

After serving in several capacities within the Shadow Cabinet, Tony Blair was appointed Shadow Home Secretary in 1992. His bond with Gordon Brown was irrevocably altered in 1994 by the abrupt death of John Smith, the leader of the Labour Party. After agreeing with Gordon Brown not to run for leadership, Tony Blair stormed to victory in the subsequent leadership race. Brown had planned to have a prominent role as chancellor in the next Labour government.

After successfully amending "Clause IV" of the Labour constitution, Tony Blair was hailed as a charismatic new breed of politician and maybe the greatest opposition leader of the modern era. The 179-vote victory for Labour in the 1997 general election came as no surprise. He was formally named prime minister on May 2, 1997, when John Major stepped down from the position.

The devolution of powers to Scotland and Wales, reforms to the House of Lords, the passage of the Human Rights Act, and the Freedom of Information Act were all significant constitutional developments that transpired rapidly. The Good Friday Agreement, which finally brought about peace in Northern Ireland in 1998, was one of his crowning accomplishments.

In terms of international relations, he came to believe that Britain had to become engaged, and in 1998 he joined the United States in attacking Iraq. In 1999, he presented his concept of "liberal interventionism" in his "Chicago" address on "The Doctrine of the International Community," and he risked a lot to defend the Kosovars. Support for Sierra Leone's democratically elected government came from a small military presence in the year 2000.

In the 2001 general election, Labour gained 167 seats, thanks to Tony Blair's leadership, a thriving economy, and the Conservative Party's dismal performance. Reforms to the public sector, such as the Prime Minister's Delivery Unit, legislation affecting Foundation Hospitals, Academy Schools, and university tuition fees, and an expanding "choice agenda," were his top priorities during his second time in office. Even though he never got around to it, he had planned to hold a referendum on Britain's adoption of the Euro.

Tony Blair's life and career were shaped by the 9/11 terrorist attacks. On the necessity to counter radical Islamism, he sided with the United States and President Bush in 2001 in Afghanistan then, more controversially, in 2003 with the invasion of Iraq.

Even though Saddam was later revealed to not have any WMD, the argument for war in the UK was based on the general perception that he had. This, together with concerns over the legitimacy of the UK's engagement and criticism of the use of government machinery, caused Tony Blair, who had previously had widespread support, to become a polarising figure.

But this aside, in 2005, under his leadership, Labour won a third consecutive general election, this time with a far lower but nevertheless substantial majority of 66 votes. The 7/7 London bombings, which were carried out by Muslim suicide bombers of British descent, prompted Blair to attempt to restrict civil freedoms, further dividing the public.

Tony Blair was heavily criticised by the Labour Party in 2006 during the Israel-Lebanon conflict for his unwillingness to oppose Israel and his unwavering support for Bush. On June 27, 2007, he tendered his resignation as prime minister.

# 60.

# IVAN THE TERRIBLE (RUSSIA)

Ivan IV, often known as Ivan the Terrible, was the most well-known of all the Muslims who lived in Moscow. Ivan IV, who ruled Russia for a lengthy period of time (1533-1584), was responsible for expanding Russian territory and making Russian culture more devout than it had ever been before. The victory that he achieved at Kazan in 1552 gave a significant blow to the Mongols and resulted in the elimination of competing centres of power such as the democratic city of Novgorod, which was located in the northern region.

In his role as the leader of a religious society, Ivan the Terrible ensured that every area of household life was ritualised via the use of semimonastic standards of behaviour. These laws were documented in a book known as the Domostrou. Over the course of the sixteenth century, the secular culture was almost eradicated as a direct result of the severe monasticization of society that occurred during this time period.

"In the beginning, Ivan was an angel. The fallen angel was represented by Ivan the Terrible. In the beginning, he was a very intelligent Tsar, but by the end, he was a demon. Additionally, Eisenstein wanted to trace this progression from angel to demon along his career. The very first photograph that he came across for this topic was of Ivan appearing in the Cathedral. And the backdrop is that this is the Last Judgement, and Ivan is still on his knees, pleading with God to pardon him. According to Naum Kleinman, a film historian, "And God remains silent when Ivan asks him, 'Have I the right to kill people for the great Russia?' and for the simple reason that silence is the answer, Ivan is attempting to kill God."

# 61.

# GAMAL ABDEL NASSER (EGYPT)

A controversial leader of the Arab world, Gamal Abdel Nasser was born on January 15, 1918, in Alexandria, Egypt, and died on September 28, 1970, in Cairo. He served as prime minister (1954–1956) and president (1956–1970) of Egypt. Nasser created the United Arab Republic (1958–1961), fought two wars with Israel (1956, 1967), and mediated the Jordanian civil war (1970).

While his father oversaw the local post office in Alexandria's Bacos neighbourhood, Nasser was born into a humble mud-brick home on an unpaved street. For many years, Egyptian official media presented the president's birthplace as Banī Murr, the rudimentary Upper Egypt town of his forefathers, in an attempt to foster a more realistic portrayal of the president as a farmer (fellahin). Upon Nasser's father's move from Alexandria, the kid received his first education in the rundown delta town of Al-Khaṭāṭibah. The next stop was Cairo, where he lived with an uncle who had just served his sentence in a British jail and who shared a block with nine other Jewish families.

Nasser was involved in several anti-British public protests and was often in conflict with schoolteachers, some of whom were British. In one of them, he took a hit to the forehead that would last a lifetime. He attended a law school for a few months after finishing high school, and then he enrolled in and graduated from the Royal Military Academy with the rank of second lieutenant.

In the Sudan, while serving in the Egyptian army, Nasser encountered three other officers: Zakaria Mohieddine, who would later become the vice president of the United Arab Republic; ʿAbd al-Ḥakīm ʿĀmir, who would later become field marshal; and Anwar el-Sādāt, who would replace Nasser as president. They conspired to depose the British and the Egyptian royal family by forming a clandestine revolutionary group called the Free Officers, the membership of which would remain unknown to everyone except Nasser.

During the Arab-Israeli War of 1948, Nasser served as an officer in one of three battalions that were encircled by Israeli forces in the Faluja Pocket, a cluster of Arab villages. ("Arab-Israeli wars" are cited).

# 62.

# PARK CHUNG-HEE (SOUTH KOREA)

The military and politician Park Chung Hee was born in Kumi, North Kyŏngsang province, Korea (now in South Korea) on September 30 or November 14, 1917, and died in Seoul, South Korea, on October 26, 1979. He served as president of the Republic of Korea (South Korea) from 1963 until his death. Although civil rights and political freedom were sacrificed during his 18-year reign, the economy expanded tremendously.

Park, who came from a poor rural family, taught elementary school after graduating with honours from Taegu (Daegu) Normal School in 1937. Having attended a Japanese military school, Park went on to serve as a second lieutenant in the Japanese army during WWII. Upon Korea's liberation from Japanese occupation, he became an officer in the Korean army. He rose through the ranks during the Korean War (1950–1953), becoming a brigadier general in 1953 and a general in 1958. He spearheaded the military revolution that deposed the Second Republic on May 16, 1961. He continued to head the junta until he was elected president of the Third Republic for the first of his three mandates two years later.

Personal liberties were curtailed, the press and opposition parties were suppressed, and Park retained control over the judiciary and universities via his programme of guided democracy at home. The National Intelligence Service, formerly known as the Korean Central Intelligence Agency (KCIA), which he established and developed became a notorious tool of political repression under his watch. According to Park, he had to do everything that he did to counter communism. He carried on the strong relationship between the United States and South Korea that his predecessors, Syngman Rhee and Yun Po Sŏn, had established in international affairs. With the programmes he launched, South Korea became one of the world's fastest-growing economies, a phenomenon known as the "economic miracle." Park had a significant role in this phenomenon.

The cruel authoritarian rule known as the Yushin ("Revitalization Reform") order was established one month after Park proclaimed martial law on October 17, 1972, with the help of a new constitution that granted him extensive powers. Political dissidents were treated with harsher and harsher severity by him. In 1979, riots and protests broke out in Korea after Park's removal of Kim Young Sam, a prominent opposition figure, from the National Assembly. Kim Jae Kyu, chief of the KCIA and a longstanding friend of Park's, had him killed.

# 63.

# KING HENRY IV (FRANCE)

Henry IV, first king of France (1589-1610) and king of Navarre (as Henry III, 1572–89), was born on December 13, 1553, in Pau, Béarn, Navarre [France], and died on May 14, 1610, in Paris, France. He converted to Roman Catholicism in 1593, at the end of the Wars of Religion, to win Paris and reunite France. He revived France's economy with the help of ministers like the Duke of Sully.

Antoine de Bourbon—Duke de Vendôme—and Jeanne d'Albret—queen of Navarre from 1555—were the parents of Henry de Bourbon-Navarre. There was only one legal line of ancestry from the French Capetian rulers, and Henry was in that line via his father. Catherine of Médicis had already given birth to three sons for the current king, Henry II, and was about to give birth to a fourth, thus it seemed almost certain that he would ascend to the French throne. Béarn was where Prince Henry spent the most of his formative years. Margaret, his future bride, was one of his second cousins who resided with the French king's children from 1561 until 1567.

A protracted civil war ensued as a result of the escalating religious tensions between Roman Catholic and Protestant (Huguenot) factions. Antoine de Bourbon briefly joined forces with the Protestants, but he later switched allegiances and died fighting for the Catholics. Henry's mother, Jeanne d'Albret, was unwavering when she came out as a Calvinist in 1560. When Henry was thirteen years old, his mother returned him to Béarn. His upbringing in the rigorous ideas of Protestantism occurred at a formative stage in his intellectual growth. At about the same time, he started training for the military. He was nominally in charge of a punishing campaign that defeated the defiant Roman Catholic nobles of lower Navarre in the fall of 1567.

As the commander of the Protestant armies in 1568, his mother entrusted him to her brother-in-law, Louis I de Bourbon, Prince de Condé. Condé was assassinated on March 13, 1569, when the Protestants were caught unawares and vanquished by the Duke d'Anjou, who would later become Henry III, at Jarnac. Upon Henry's introduction by Jeanne d'Albret, the young prince received his military training from Gaspard de Coligny, the newly appointed chief of the Protestant soldiers. Henry was a standout in the Huguenot cavalry attack that led to the initial charge at the Battle of Arnay-le-Duc on June 26, 1570. He reflected on the destruction that had befallen the kingdom and was instilled with a soldierly spirit that would last a lifetime throughout the protracted struggle that spanned the devastated provinces, from Poitou to the very centre of Burgundy.

# 64.

# NICOLAE CEAUȘESCU (ROMANIA)

Born Nicolae Ceaușescu on January 26, 1918, in Scornicești, Romania, he was a Communist politician and the leader of Romania from 1965 until his downfall and death in the revolution of 1989. He died on December 25, 1989, near Bucharest.

In 1936 and 1940, Ceaușescu was imprisoned for his activity inside the Communist Party. He was a part of the Romanian Communist youth movement in the early 1930s. He wed Communist activist Elena Petrescu in 1939. Ceaușescu became a protege of Communist leader Gheorghe Gheorghiu-Dej while in jail; Gheorghiu-Dej would go on to become Romania's unchallenged Communist leader starting in 1952. After Ceaușescu escaped from jail in August 1944, just before Romania was occupied by the Soviets, he was secretary of the Union of Communist Youth (1944–1945). He was charge of the Romanian Ministry of Agriculture from 1948 to 1950 when the Communists fully took control in the country in 1947. From 1950 to 1954, he was a major general serving as deputy minister of the armed forces. Ceaușescu rose through the ranks of the party under

Gheorghiu-Dej and finally became a prominent figure in the Politburo and Secretariat, holding the position of second-in-command.

Following Gheorghiu-Dej's death in March 1965, Ceaușescu took over as first secretary of the Romanian Communist Party (he had been general secretary since July 1965). In December 1967, he also became head of state after becoming the chair of the State Council. As he boldly opposed the Soviet Union's hegemony over Romania, he quickly gained public support for his autonomous, nationalist political path. Ceaușescu strongly opposed the 1968 invasion of Czechoslovakia by Warsaw Pact troops and the 1979 Soviet invasion of Afghanistan, therefore ending Romania's active involvement in the alliance during that decade (1979). The position of president of Romania was established in 1974, and Ceaușescu was elected to it.

Although Ceaușescu maintained a policy of independence in international affairs, he drew more and closer to the communist ideology of central planning in his domestic government. No internal criticism or dissent was permitted by his secret police, who imposed strict restrictions over free speech and the media. Ceaușescu enacted Decree 770, which essentially banned abortion and contraception, in 1966 in an effort to increase Romania's population. While doctors kept an eye on reproductive-age women to make sure they weren't trying to limit their fertility, the number of maternal deaths surged as women sought out illegal and dangerous ways to end their pregnancies. Ceaușescu ordered the sale of a considerable portion of the agricultural and industrial output of the nation in 1982 in an attempt to settle the substantial foreign debt that his administration had accrued due to its botched economic endeavours in the 1970s. Discontent and a decline in living conditions were exacerbated by the subsequent severe scarcity of food, gasoline, electricity, medications, and other essentials. Additionally, Ceaușescu elevated several members of his extended family to prominent positions within the party and administration, including his wife Elena, and established a pervasive personality cult. An ambitious and unrealistic goal of his was to relocate the inhabitants of hundreds of Romanian villages to so-called agrotechnical centres by demolishing them.

The proclamation by Ceaușescu to open fire on antigovernment protesters in Timișoara on December 17, 1989, led to the downfall of his dictatorship. Protests reached Bucharest on December 22, and a contingent of the Romanian army betrayed the protestors. The military troops apprehended and detained Ceaușescu and his wife on the very same day that they left the city in a helicopter. In a hasty trial that began on December 25, a special military tribunal found the pair guilty of many offences, including mass murder. A firing squad subsequently shot Ceaușescu and his wife.

# 65.

# JUSTINIAN I (BYZANTINE EMPIRE)

From 527 to 565 CE, Justinian I was emperor of the Byzantine Empire. His uncle, Emperor Justin I, was a bodyguard for the emperor and succeeded to the throne when Anastasius died in 518 CE; he was born in the Illyrian hamlet of Tauresium in 482 CE. Among the most influential rulers of the late Roman and Byzantine eras, Justinian stands out. Between 533 and 534 CE, he launched a major military effort to recover Africa from the Vandals, and between 535 and 554 CE, he retook Italy from the Goths. In 532 CE, he also began the reconstruction of the Hagia Sophia cathedral, and across the empire, new churches, monasteries, forts, water reservoirs, and bridges were built according to his orders. The codification of the legal changes contained in the Corpus Juris Civilis, which he oversaw between 529 and 534 CE, was his other notable accomplishment. From the reign of Emperor Hadrian (117–138 CE) up till the current day, all of the Roman laws have been compiled into this. A lot of people think he was one of the best (and most divisive) emperors of the late Roman and Byzantine era.

The details of Justinian's childhood are sketchy at best. His mother, Vigilantia, was an imperial bodyguard and the sister of the Excubitor. To ensure his nephew's education, Justin took him in as his own and sent him to Constantinople. Throughout Justin's tenure, Justinian was a trusted counsellor and confidant; in 521 CE, he was appointed Consul, and thereafter, he oversaw the Eastern army. He wed Theodora, an impoverished lady who may have been a prostitute, around 525 CE.

Justinian, who was not a combatant in and of himself, nonetheless launched a massive military campaign to conquer Sicily, Africa, and Italy. But he started his military career in the east. The Sassanian Empire and the Kingdom of Iberia, located in the Caucasus Mountains (around the present-day Georgia), were at odds during the Iberian War (526–532 CE). The fight against the Sassanian Empire began with Anastasius I and continued throughout this conflict. When Sassanian Shah (emperor) Kavadh I died and his son Khosroes I took the throne, a peace was negotiated after many conflicts.

# 66.

# CHARLES DE GAULLE (FRANCE)

In addition to being a French soldier, politician, and architect of France's Fifth Republic, Charles de Gaulle was born on November 22, 1890 in Lille, France, and passed away on November 9, 1970 in Colombey-les-Deux-Églises. It was in 1913 that he enlisted in the military, and he served with distinction throughout World War I. In the year 1925, he was given a position on the senior staff of the Supreme War Council. His promotion to brigadier general occurred in 1940, and he also held the position of undersecretary of state for defence under Paul Reynaud for a short period of time. Following the successful invasion and occupation of France by the Germans, he fled to England and initiated the Free French organisation. He travelled to Algiers in 1943 and became president of the French Committee of National Liberation, first in collaboration with Henri-Honoré Giraud. He was devoted to France and committed to the liberation of the country. After Paris was freed from French occupation, he returned to the city and led two interim administrations until finally resigning in 1946. As a result of his opposition to the Fourth Republic, he established the Rally of the

French People (RPF) in 1947. However, he broke his ties to the latter organisation in 1953. After leaving the public eye, he concentrated on writing his memoirs. In 1958, he returned to office as prime minister with the authority to alter the constitution. This was in response to the fact that an uprising in Algeria had the potential to bring about civil war in France. He was elected president of the newly formed Fifth Republic in the same year, which insured that he would have a powerful presidency. His actions brought an end to the Algerian War and resulted in the formation of twelve sovereign republics from France's African territory. His position of neutrality during the Vietnam War was seen by many as anti-Americannism, and he withdrew France from the North Atlantic Treaty Organisation (NATO). He initiated a strategy of détente with nations that were part of the Iron Curtain and travelled extensively in order to establish a connection with countries that spoke French. Following the social disturbance that occurred in May 1968, which was caused by students and workers, he was unsuccessful in a referendum on constitutional revisions and withdrew from his position in 1969.

# 67.

# EMPEROR QIN SHI HUANG (CHINA)

At the time period of Shi Huang (259-210 B.C.), there is a person who is regarded with both respect and revulsion in China. He was the first man to unite China and the first Emperor of China, but he was also a tyrant whose tyrannical rule caused him to be loathed for years after his death. He was the first man to unify China. In addition to being the genius behind the building of the Terracotta Army, he also gave the order to build what would later become the Great Wall himself. His all-consuming avarice, on the other hand, caused the country's resources to be devastated, and it is said that under his reign, the population of China decreased by more than half. Due to the fact that he was so reviled by his own people, he was the focus of many failed efforts to kill him. One of these attempts served as the impetus for the martial arts epic Hero, which starred Jet-Li. The Qin The ascent to power of Shi Huang and the establishment of his empire, although being cruel and ruthless, has unquestionably become the stuff of legends.

In relation to the birth of Qin Shi Huang, there is a great deal of disagreement. The name Ying Zheng was bestowed upon him at the time of his birth in the year 259 B.C. in the city of Handan. His father, Yiren, was the Qin prince, and he was the oldest son. According to Yiren, his mother was the Lady of Zhao, who was a cherished concubine.

Prior to the birth of Ying Zheng, his father Yiren was allegedly being kept as a captive by the State of Zhao. He was rescued by a rich trader by the name of Lu Buwei. Following this, Yiren became King Zhuangxiang of Qin and succeeded to the throne. The historian Sima Qian[1] indicates that Lu Buwei was the one who introduced Yiren to Zhao Ji, who was Ying Zhen's mother. But Yiren was unaware of the fact that Zhao Ji had been Lu Buwei's concubine for a considerable amount of time and was carrying his kid at the time. There was an allegation going around that Ying Zheng was in reality Lu Buwei's son who was not legitimately born. The possibility that Ying Zheng was not legitimate was widely thought across China at the time, which added to the bad opinion that many people held of him. According to contemporary research, it is likely that Sima Qian included this story in his records in order to smear Ying Zheng. This is because, in accordance with the ideas of Confucianism, merchants such as Lu Buwei were considered to be among the lowest of the social classes.

# 68.

# BILL CLINTON (USA)

Peace and economic prosperity were at an all-time high for the United States during President William Jefferson Clinton's tenure. After FDR, he became the first Democratic president to secure a second term in office. He may mention the nation's record-lowest inflation rate in 30 years, record-highest homeownership rate, falling crime rates in various regions, and shrinking assistance rolls. He succeeded in creating a surplus while proposing the first balanced budget in many decades. In an effort to commemorate the turn of the century, Clinton proposed a massive nationwide campaign to eradicate racism.

After his massive health care reform programme collapsed in his second year in office, Clinton changed gears and said, "the era of big government is over." He pushed for stricter gun control laws, better educational standards, employment protection for parents who had to stay home with ill children, and more environmental regulations.

William Jefferson Blythe III Clinton came into this world in Hope, Arkansas on August 19, 1946, only three months after his father passed away in a car crash. Roger Clinton of Hot Springs, Arkansas, was his father. His mother wed him when he was four years old. Upon entering high school, he assumed the surname of his maternal side.

He thought about making a living as a musician after achieving academic and musical success on the saxophone. In the Rose Garden of the White House, he met President John F. Kennedy while serving as a high school delegate to Boys Nation. He decided to devote his life to helping others after that event.

Clinton received a Rhodes Scholarship to attend Oxford University in 1968 after graduating from Georgetown University. In 1973, he became involved in Arkansas politics after earning a law degree from Yale University.

He ran for the United States Congress in 1974 but lost the race for Arkansas's Third District. Hillary Rodham, who had earned degrees from both Wellesley and Yale Law School, was his bride the following year. Chelsea was born in 1980; she was their only child.

In 1976, Clinton was chosen to serve as the attorney general of Arkansas. In 1978, she was elected governor. He was out of government for two terms, but returned four years later and remained in that position until he was defeated by George Bush and Ross Perot in the 1992 presidential campaign.

Senator Albert Gore Jr. of Tennessee, who was 44 years old at the time, and Clinton were the leaders of a new age in American politics. A unified political party has controlled both houses of Congress and the presidency for the first time in twelve years. That advantage, however, was short-lived, as Republicans went on to win control of both chambers of Congress in 1994.

Clinton became the second sitting U.S. president to be impeached in 1998 after scandals involving his affairs with a White House intern erupted. He was acquitted of all allegations after a trial in the Senate. Even after apologising to the country, he maintained record-high levels of public support for his presidency.

On a global scale, he was instrumental in sending peacekeepers to a war-torn Bosnia and in dropping bombs on Iraq after Saddam Hussein blocked UN inspections for chemical, biological, and nuclear weapons.

He gained international prominence as an advocate for freer trade, a stronger North Atlantic Treaty Organisation, and a crackdown on drug trafficking. His advocacy of American-style freedom brought him massive audiences as he travelled around China, Russia, Africa, and South America.

# 69.

# LEONID BREZHNEV (USSR)

Ukrainian mining town Kamensk was the birthplace of Leonid Ilyich Brezhnev, the future leader of one of the world's two most powerful countries. His parents were Russian. Almost little is known about his formative years; however, he did begin working at his father's steel factory when he was fifteen years old.

Following the Russian Revolution, Brezhnev became a land surveyor after pursuing a technical degree. Joining the Communist Party in 1931 and going on to hold a number of local party positions, his political aspirations were quickly made clear. The youthful apparatchik shown an impressive talent for accurately assessing the political scene. Brezhnev, in his role as first secretary of the Communist Party in Kazakstan, helped the new Soviet premier, Nikita Khrushchev, with his "Virgin Lands" agricultural campaign after Stalin's death. Brezhnev also supported Khrushchev during an unsuccessful coup d'état. Brezhnev was soon elevated to the rank of full Politburo member.

He was considered the frontrunner to succeed Khrushchev in the early 1960s. In 1960, he was appointed chairman of the Supreme Soviet Praesidium. In 1964, he resigned to take a position as second secretary of the Central Committee, directly assisting Khrushchev. But Khrushchev was disappointed with the help he gave. Even though he had only been in office for three months, Brezhnev was instrumental in leading the conservative alliance that deposed Khrushchev.

After Khrushchev was removed from office, Brezhnev personally reaped many benefits. He became one of the two most influential persons in the Soviet Union after being named first secretary of the Communist Party. Premier Aleksei Kosygin was the other. But Brezhnev became the undisputed leader and Communist Party general secretary in due time.

In stark contrast to Khrushchev's energetic and often chaotic rule, Brezhnev's leadership style was colourless. The enormous Soviet bureaucracy, which had been threatened by Khrushchev's reforms, found this comforting. Government power centres like the KGB recovered the authority—if not nearly the brutality—they had enjoyed during Stalin's period under Brezhnev, and the Soviet bureaucracy prospered.

An early indication of Brezhnev's worldview was the Soviet decision to invade Czechoslovakia in 1968 to suppress the Prague Spring. As part of his speech that defended the action, he laid out the now-famous "Brezhnev Doctrine," which affirmed Moscow's authority to meddle in the internal affairs of other communist nations.

The Cold War with the United States was Brezhnev's life's work, and he was a devoted Cold Warrior. He was more circumspect than Khrushchev, but he nonetheless backed left-leaning governments and U.S. enemies all over the globe, especially in Vietnam, the Middle East, and the Third World. In 1972, Brezhnev and Nixon signed the SALT accord, which froze certain U.S. and Soviet military systems, marking the beginning of a new age of detente. However, the new age was plagued by persistent Cold War animosities, which led to its brief lifespan. By 1979, it had become little more than a distant memory, when Brezhnev and his colleagues sanctioned the Soviet invasion of Afghanistan.

Brezhnev had become an ageing, frail elderly man at this point. The Soviet economy collapsed along with Brezhnev's health. Years of disproportionate investment in defence and aerospace at the price of other economic areas, like as agriculture, have taken their toll. Long lineups formed for everyday Soviet inhabitants to receive food and medicine, and the country's economy and level of life declined gradually but steadily.

The Soviet Union itself had less than a decade to survive when Brezhnev passed away at the age of 75 on November 10, 1982.

# 70.

# YITZHAK RABIN (ISRAEL)

Israeli politician and soldier Yitzhak Rabin was born on March 1, 1922, in Jerusalem, and died on November 4, 1995, in Tel Aviv-Yafo, Israel. He was prime minister of Israel from 1974 to 1977 and from 1992 to 1995, during which time he guided Israel towards peace with its Arab and Palestinian neighbours. During the Six-Day War (June 1967), he oversaw the Israeli military as chief of staff. In 1994, Rabin was awarded the Nobel Prize for Peace with Shimon Peres, his foreign minister, and Yasser Arafat, leader of the Palestine Liberation Organisation (PLO).

After finishing agricultural school in Kadoorie in Kefar Tavor, Rabin enlisted in the Palmach, a Haganah commando organisation, in 1941. While in Syria and Lebanon, he took part in operations against the Vichy French. He battled Egyptians in the Negev and oversaw operations near Jerusalem during the first Arab-Israeli War (1948–49). His ideas for the Six-Day War winning tactics—a rapid mobilisation of reserves and the ground destruction of enemy aircraft—came during his time as chief of staff in January 1964, after graduating (1953) from the British military college. He gained national renown as a potential guarantor of Israel's security after being largely regarded as the war hero by the Israeli people.

After Rabin retired from the army in 1968, he became Israel's ambassador to the US, where he established strong relationships with American officials and secured cutting-edge American military systems for Israel. As a member of a broader Middle East peace solution, he called for Israeli departure from Arab lands seized in the 1967 war, which angered Israeli hard-liners.

Rabin got involved in Israeli politics after returning to the country in March 1973. He became a member of Prime Minister Golda Meir's cabinet in March 1974 after being elected to the Knesset (parliament) in December as a member of the Labour Party. Following Meir's resignation in April 1974, Rabin took over as party leader and became the fifth prime minister of Israel, the first to be born in the country, in June. A cease-fire with Syria in the Golan Heights and a daring raid at Entebbe, Uganda, in July 1976 involving the rescue of Israeli and other hostages from an aircraft hijacked by members of the Popular Front for the Liberation of Palestine and the Red Army Faction (a West German extreme leftist group) were both accomplished during his tenure as Israel's leader, which demonstrated his readiness to negotiate with enemies and take decisive action when needed. Among his many lasting legacies as prime minister, the 1975 Interim deal with Egypt stands out. It was this deal that set the stage for the 1979 permanent peace treaty between Egypt and Israel.

In May 1977, a general election was called by Rabin due to his forced resignation as prime minister and leader of the Labour Party in April. This was in response to revelations that he and his wife had kept bank accounts in the US, which was against Israeli law. Party leader Shimon Peres succeeded him.

# 71.

# EMPEROR HIROHITO (JAPAN)

From 1926 until his death in 1989, Hirohito reigned as emperor of Japan. He was born on April 29, 1901, in Tokyo, Japan, and died on January 7, 1989, in the same city. He remained in power for longer than any other king in Japan.

The Aoyama Palace in Tokyo was the site of Hirohito's birth. He was the son of the Taishō emperor and the grandson of the Meiji emperor. He attended both the Peers' School and the Crown Prince's Institute for his education. He published extensively on marine biology, a subject that piqued his attention at an early age. Being the first crown prince of Japan to go overseas, he made a historic trip to Europe in 1921. His father's retirement due to mental illness bestowed the title of prince regent upon him upon his return. Princess Nagako Kuni was married to Hirohito in 1924.

On December 25, 1926, after his father's death, Hirohito became emperor of Japan. Shōwa, meaning "Bright Peace" or "Enlightened Harmony," was the name given to his rule. Although the emperor possessed absolute power according to the Meiji Constitution (promulgated in 1889), in reality, he often agreed with the policies proposed by his advisors and ministers. On rare occasions, nevertheless, he made his power known, most famously in February 1936, when he ordered the repression of a coup plotted by many military commanders.

From the early 1930s until the conclusion of World War II in 1945, Japan was militarily active, and historians disagree on how Hirohito was responsible for this time. According to many, he strongly opposed going to war with the US and the Axis Powers' alliance between Germany and Italy, but he felt pressured to comply by the militarists who were gaining control of the military and the administration. From the Japanese invasion of Manchuria (now northeastern China) in 1931 to the conclusion of the war, some historians believe that Hirohito was heavily engaged in the planning of Japan's expansionist objectives. Some people think that both of those explanations are correct, while others think that the truth is in the middle.

However, Hirohito resolved the disagreement in favour of the peace-seekers in August 1945, when Japan was on the verge of defeat and its leaders were split over whether to surrender or to fiercely defend the home islands from an impending invasion by the Allied Powers. By making a nationwide radio broadcast to proclaim Japan's acceptance of the conditions of capitulation proposed by the Allies on August 15, he broke the norm of imperial silence. On January 1, 1946, Hirohito made a second historic broadcast in which he rejected the customary quasi-divine position of Japan's rulers.

The United States imposed a constitutional monarchy on Japan in 1947 after drafting a new constitution for the nation in 1946. The authority was greatly limited, and the emperor no longer had any real say in matters of state. With this title came the honour of being called the "symbol of the state and of the unity of the people." The Japanese emperor Hirohito made a concerted effort to humanise the royal family by allowing photos and anecdotes about his life and family to be published and by making frequent public appearances. Both the popularity of Hirohito and the stability of the Japanese imperial system were bolstered by these measures.

Crown Prince Akihito broke a 1,500-year tradition in 1959 when he married commoner Shōda Michiko, his eldest son. Hirohito became the first reigning Japanese emperor to go overseas in 1971, breaking yet another precedent with his trip of Europe. On his 1975 official visit to the US, he visited Disneyland in southern California—a much-publicized excursion—and met with President Richard M. Nixon, the first American president and Japanese emperor to ever meet. Akihito succeeded Hirohito as emperor after the latter's death in 1989.

# 72.

# DAVID BEN-GURION (ISRAEL)

In spite of America's backing for the Balfour Declaration of 1917—which advocated for a Jewish national home in Palestine—President Franklin D. Roosevelt had promised Arabs in 1945 that America would exercise restraint in the region until both the Jews and the Arabs were consulted. Until May 1948, the British had a colonial mandate over Palestine. They were against the establishment of two separate states in Palestine, one Arab and one Jewish, and they were also against the unrestricted immigration of Jewish refugees to the area. By maintaining cordial ties with the Arab world, Britain hoped to safeguard its strategically important economic and political interests in Palestine.

President Truman recruited many specialists to investigate the Palestinian question shortly after he became office. Truman formed a special cabinet committee in the summer of 1946, with Assistant Secretary of State Dr. Henry F. Grady serving as chairman. This group began discussions with a similar British committee to address the fate of Palestine. After openly endorsing the establishment of a Jewish state in October of 1946, Truman stated in May of the same year that he had approved a proposal to let 100,000 displaced people into Palestine. The UN Special Commission on Palestine studied the Palestinian issue in 1947 and suggested dividing Palestine into two states, one Arab and one Jewish. Resolution 181, sometimes called the Partition Resolution, was enacted by the United Nations on November 29, 1947. It was intended to split the former Palestinian mandate of Great Britain into Jewish and Arab governments in May 1948, when the British mandate was due to expire. The resolution stipulates that the religiously significant territory around Jerusalem should continue to be a corpus separatum governed by the United Nations on an international level.

U.S. Department of State officials advocated for a UN trusteeship with immigration restrictions for Jews and the partition of Palestine into Jewish & Arab provinces rather than nations, even though the US supported Resolution 181. The State Department cautioned against American involvement in support of the Jewish people due to concerns about the possible expansion of Soviet influence in the Arab world and the chance that Arab oil-producing states might limit U.S. oil supply. An all-out war in Palestine became a growing worry for the Department of State as the deadline for the British withdrawal from Palestine drew closer. Arab governments had promised to strike almost immediately after the UN approved the partition resolution, and this danger persisted even after the resolution was enacted.

Truman chose to recognise Israel as a state despite the Department of State endorsing a trusteeship and the escalating violence between Palestinian Arabs & Palestinian Jews.

# 73.

# FRANCISCO FRANCO (SPAIN)

Francisco Franco (born December 4, 1892, El Ferrol, Spain—died November 20, 1975, Madrid) was the general and leader of the Nationalist forces that overthrew the Spanish democratic republic in the Spanish Civil War (1936–39). He was Spain's head of state until 1975 and head of government until 1973.

The Galician seaside city and naval centre of El Ferrol was Franco's birthplace. Franco's father, a Spanish Naval Administrative Corps commander, was eccentric, extravagant, and dissolute. Franco was close to his religious, conservative upper middle-class Roman Catholic mother and more disciplined than other boys his age. Franco was supposed to become a navy officer like four ancestors and his older brother, but navy Academy enrollment were reduced, forcing him to join the army. He joined Toledo's Infantry Academy aged 14 in 1907 and graduated three years later.

Franco was moved to Spanish Morocco in 1912 at age 19 after volunteering for active service in the colonial battles that began in

1909. He became a first lieutenant in an elite Moroccan cavalry unit the following year. Young Franco immediately proved his ability to lead soldiers and earned a reputation for professionalism at a period when many Spanish commanders were sloppy and unprofessional. He carefully planned his unit's tactics and paid more attention to the soldiers' well-being than usual. He was honest, reclusive, and had few close friends, therefore he avoided frivolous activities. He became the youngest Spanish army captain in 1915. He went to Spain to heal after being shot in the abdomen the following year. He was appointed second in command of the newly formed Spanish Foreign Legion in 1920 and took over in 1923. That year, he married Carmen Polo and had a daughter. The legion helped quell the Moroccan uprising in important battles. Franco was elevated to brigadier general aged 33 in 1926 after becoming a national hero. at 1928, he became director of the newly founded General Military Academy at Saragossa.

After the monarchy fell in 1931, the new Spanish Republic authorities instituted a much-needed military reform, which interrupted Franco's career. Franco became inactive once the General Military Academy was disbanded. Franco accepted the new rule and his temporary relegation with exemplary discipline, despite being a monarchist and gentlemen of the king's chamber. Franco was reinstated in 1933 and elevated to major general in 1934 when conservative forces took over the nation. Franco quells a brutal Asturian miners' insurrection in October 1934 against three conservative government members. Success in this operation elevated him. He became head of the Spanish army's general staff in May 1935 and tightened discipline and strengthened military institutions, although he left many changes in place.

Parliament was dissolved and fresh elections were scheduled for February 1936 after scandals undermined the Radicals, a coalition party. By then, the Spanish political parties had divided into the rightist National Bloc and the leftist Popular Front. The left won the elections, but the new administration failed to stop Spain's social and economic collapse. Franco had never joined a political party, but the instability drove him to ask the government for a state of emergency. After his appeal was denied, he was demoted from the general staff to a remote Canary Island command. As the political system collapsed, he joined the rebels after first refusing to join a military plot against the government.

# 74.

# ALEXANDER HAMILTON (USA)

Alexander Hamilton, a prominent figure in the establishment of the United States, actively participated in the American Revolutionary War, contributed to the creation of the Constitution, and held the esteemed position of the first secretary of the treasury. He established and served as the principal designer of the financial system in the United States.

Hamilton was born on January 11, perhaps in 1755 or 1757, in Charlestown, located on the British island of Nevis. Hamilton's parents, Rachel Faucette and James Hamilton, were unmarried at the time of his birth. James deserted the family in 1766 and Rachel passed away in 1768. During his teenage years, Hamilton resided in the Danish territory of St. Croix. Hamilton's exceptional intellect became evident to the local community when he wrote a persuasive letter detailing the impact of a storm on the island. As a result, they gathered funds to finance his education in the British North American colonies.

Hamilton landed in mainland America in late 1772 and first sought admission to the College of New Jersey (current Princeton). However, he ultimately decided to enrol at King's College in New York City. During his time in New York, Hamilton actively endorsed and backed the colonial demonstrations against British imperial policies. In 1774 and 1775, he authored many pamphlets that criticised the opinions of the vocal loyalist Samuel Seabury. Hamilton engaged in military training with a group of volunteers in 1775 and was appointed as the captain of an artillery company in March 1776. During the American Revolutionary War, he actively participated in the battles of Kip's Bay, White Plains, Trenton, and Princeton.

The youthful captain made a strong impression on higher-ranking commanders in the Continental Army, prompting William Alexander (Lord Stirling) to request Hamilton's services as his military assistant. On January 25, 1777, the Pennsylvania Evening Post published an advertising stating that Captain Alexander Hamilton, belonging to the New-York company of artillery, may perhaps benefit by contacting the printer of the newspaper.1 General George Washington extended an invitation to Hamilton to join his military staff, which Hamilton willingly accepted, resulting in his appointment as a lieutenant colonel. During the subsequent four-year period, Hamilton served as one of Washington's most esteemed aides, doing a diverse range of duties such as composing correspondence sent to Congress, state officials, and fellow commanders of the Continental Army.

# 75.

# MIKHAIL GORBACHEV (USSR)

Mikhail Gorbachev, a Soviet statesman, served as the general secretary of the Communist Party of the Soviet Union (CPSU) from 1985 to 1991 and as the president of the Soviet Union from 1990 to 1991. He was born on March 2, 1931, in Privolnoye, Stavropol kray, Russia, U.S.S.R., and passed away on August 30, 2022, in Moscow, Russia. His attempts to establish a democratic political system and distribute economic power resulted in the collapse of communism and the disintegration of the Soviet Union in 1991. Gorbachev was given the Nobel Prize for Peace in 1990, partly due to his role in ending the Soviet Union's postwar control over eastern Europe.

Early life Gorbachev was born to Russian peasants in the Stavropol area (kray) in the southwestern region of Russia. In 1946, he became a member of the Komsomol, the Young Communist League, and worked as a combine harvester operator at a state farm in Stavropol for the next four years. He shown great potential as a Komsomol member, and in 1952 he enrolled in the law department at Moscow State University and joined the Communist Party. In 1955, he successfully completed his legal degree and then held various positions in the Komsomol and regular party organisations in Stavropol. Eventually, he achieved the position of first secretary of the regional party committee in 1970.

In 1971, Mikhail Gorbachev was appointed as a member of the Central Committee of the Communist Party of the Soviet Union (CPSU). In 1979–80, Gorbachev became a member of the Politburo, the highest decision-making body of the CPSU. In 1985, he was chosen as the general secretary of the CPSU. In October 1988, General Secretary Gorbachev assumed the position of chairman of the praesidium of the national legislature, also known as the Supreme Soviet. Soon after, Gorbachev reorganised the Soviet government to include a bicameral parliament. In 1989, the parliament selected a new Supreme Soviet among its members and appointed Gorbachev as its leader. In 1990, Gorbachev ran unopposed for the presidency of the Soviet Union.

# 76.

# AUGUSTO PINOCHET (CHILE)

A military from Chile, Augusto Pinochet (1915–2006) took power in a brutal coup in September 1973. Pinochet, who was born into a middle-class family in the seaside town of Valparaiso, attended a military academy after finishing high school and graduated in 1936. After being appointed to the rank of lieutenant in the Chilean infantry, he embarked on a career in the military. Despite never having seen battle or active duty, Pinochet ascended through the ranks. He assumed the position of commander of a prison camp for individuals with communist sympathies in 1953. Afterwards, he spent time in Chile and Ecuador at military institutions, where he taught and studied. After being elevated to the rank of general in 1971, Pinochet was named chief of staff of the army the following year. President Salvador Allende of Chile nominated Pinochet to head the Chilean military in August 1973. With the implicit approval of the CIA and other right-wing politicians and military leaders, Pinochet launched a military coup the month after. The government was overthrown and Allende was killed, most likely by suicide, as a result of this coup.

Pinochet became a fascist military dictator after ruling Chile for a year as leader of a military junta. After Pinochet's coup, the US gave his administration about $400 million in loans and help. In addition, Pinochet's secret police, the Dirección de Inteligencia Nacional (DINA), received material and training from the CIA. As Pinochet's rule over Chile tightened, he persecuted his political opponents to the point that hundreds were either killed or disappeared without a trace. To Pinochet, they were all "communists," even though most of his detractors and victims belonged to more moderate socialist, social democratic, and liberal camps. In the late 1970s, investigations of Pinochet's human rights violations in Chile were heavily reported and examined. In order to attract businesses and investors from across the world, the new government in Chile enacted sweeping economic reforms at home. This revived the economy, although unemployment and poverty worsened throughout Pinochet's presidency.

A number of years of domestic and international calls for democratic change led to Pinochet's ouster in 1990. Pope John Paul II likewise pushed the Chilean dictator to loosen his hold and permit democratic change during his April 1987 visit. The vote that Pinochet consented to in October 1988 essentially broke his totalitarian rule. Following Pinochet's removal from office in March 1990, the nation started its transition to democracy. The elderly ex-dictator went to Britain in 1998 for specialised medical treatment. For his role in approving the 1970s assassinations and tortures of Spanish citizens and diplomats, he was apprehended in October 1988. British officials made the contentious conclusion that the former dictator could not be extradited to Spain to face punishment, despite the fact that they had been Pinochet's friends throughout his reign. Pinochet was instead given immunity from prosecution and returned to Chile. Although Pinochet's immunity was abolished in 2004, he passed away in December 2006, preventing the laying of charges. Evidence of political assassinations, extensive torture, corruption, tax evasion, and money laundering has been found in subsequent investigations of Pinochet's tenure as president.

# 77.

# EMPEROR AKBAR (MUGHAL EMPIRE)

The greatest Mughal emperor of India, Akbar, was born on October 15, 1542, in Umarkot (now in Sindh province, Pakistan), and died on October 25, 1605, at Agra. He established Mughal dominion across the majority of the Indian subcontinent during his reign (1556–1605). In an effort to keep his empire together, Akbar instituted policies that would win over the non-Muslim citizens of his domain. He restructured tax collecting, consolidated his financial system, and reinforced his central administration. Even though he never denied Islam, he was very interested in other faiths and encouraged Muslims, Parsis, Christians, and Hindus to have religious discussions with him. Despite his own lack of literacy, he made his court a cultural hub by supporting academics, poets, artists, and musicians.

The political elites of northern India in the Middle Ages were mostly composed of Turks, Mongols, and Iranians, all of whom Abū al-Fatḥ Jalāl al-Dīn Muḥammad Akbar was a descendant of. Genghis Khan and Timur (Tamerlane) were among his forebears. In a fruitless attempt to assert his dominion over the Sindh area (now Sindh province, Pakistan), his father Humāyūn was expelled from Delhi, his capital, by the Afghan invader Shēr Shah of Sūr. The shah loaned Humāyūn forces, so he soon had to go from India for Afghanistan and Iran. Ten years after Shēr Shah's demise, in 1555, Humāyūn reclaimed his kingdom. Currently inhabited by Punjab state in India and Punjab province in Pakistan, Akbar was appointed ruler of the Punjab area when he was thirteen years old.

In 1556, Humāyūn passed away just as he was beginning to solidify his power. Hemu, a Hindu minister, claimed the crown for himself within a few months, and his governors lost control of numerous major towns, including Delhi itself. But in the Second Battle of Panipat (near present-day Panipat, Haryana state, India), a Mughal army defeated Hemu on November 5, 1556, so establishing Akbar's succession and controlling the path to Delhi.

Following the advice of his chief minister, Bayram Khan, Akbar's power was progressively solidified and expanded; yet, upon his arrival, his reign barely included the Punjab and the region around Delhi. After Akbar retired Bayram Khan in 1560 and took over as ruler, the practise proceeded, first with household influences but later as an absolute king.

# 78.

# RICHARD THE LIONHEART (UK)

Between the years 1189 and 1199, Richard I reigned as King of England. He was born on September 8, 1157, and passed away on April 6, 1199. During the same time period, he also held the titles of "Duke of Normandy, Aquitaine, and Gascony, Lord of Cyprus, Count of Poitiers, Anjou, Maine, and Nantes, and overlord of Brittany" at different points in time. In spite of the fact that he was the third of five sons born to King Henry II of England and Duchess Eleanor of Aquitaine, it seemed that he would not succeed to the throne. However, all of his brothers, with the exception of John, had already passed away before their father. Because of his reputation as a strong military commander and fighter, Richard is also known as Richard the Lionheart or Richard Coeur de Lion (Norman French: Le quor de lion). Both of these names come from mediaeval French.(1) [1] In addition, the troubador Bertran de Born referred to him as Richard Oc-e-Non, which is an Occitan word that means "Yes and No." This may have been due to his reputation for being terse.2

Richard, who was just sixteen years old at the time, had already assumed leadership of his own army and put down rebellions in Poitou that were led by his father.Although he finalised a peace treaty and ended the campaign without retaking Jerusalem, Richard was an important Christian commander during the Third Crusade. He led the campaign after Philip II of France left, and he achieved considerable victories against Saladin, his Muslim counterpart. Despite this, he did not succeed in retaking Jerusalem.

It is likely that Richard was fluent in both French and Occitan. He was born in England, and he spent his youth there. However, before to becoming king, he spent the most of his adult life in the Duchy of Aquitaine, which is located in the southwest of France. In the years immediately after his succession, Charles remained in England for a relatively little period of time, maybe as little as six months. It was during his reign that he spent the most of his time either on Crusade, in prison, or vigorously defending his territories in France. It is said that he would rather utilise his kingdom as a source of cash to sustain his forces than as a duty that requires his presence as ruler. This is because he does not consider his kingdom to be a responsibility that requires his attendance. The people who were under his rule, however, saw him as a religious hero. He is still one of the few kings of England who is remembered more often by his epithet than by his regnal number, and he is a character who has endured as an iconic figure in both England and France.

# 79.

# AYATOLLAH KHOMEINI (IRAN)

He was an Iranian Shi'i cleric who led the revolution that overthrew Mohammad Reza Shah Pahlavi in 1979 (see Iranian Revolution) and who served as Iran's ultimate political and religious authority for the subsequent ten years. Ruhollah Khomeini was born on September 24, 1902 (see Researcher's Note), in Khomeyn, Iran, and passed away on June 3, 1989, in Tehrān.

Childhood and involvement in clerical activism

He was the grandson and son of mullahs, who are religious leaders who adhere to the Shi'i faith. On the instructions of a local landowner, his father was murdered when he was around five months old. After his mother and aunt passed away, his older brother Mortaza, who would later become known as Ayatollah Pasandideh, took on the responsibility of raising the young Khomeini that he had been nurtured by. He received his education from a number of Islamic institutions, and around the year 1922, he made his home in the city of Qom, which is considered to be Iran's intellectual capital for Shiʿi academia. He became a distinguished scholar there in the

1930s and became recognised by the name of his hometown, Khomayn (sometimes spelt Khomeyn or Khomen). He received this moniker from his hometown. While Khomeini was a Shi'i scholar and teacher, he produced a multitude of writings on Islamic philosophy, law, and ethics. However, it was his outspoken opposition to Mohammad Reza Shah Pahlavi, Iran's ruler, as well as his denunciations of Western influences and his uncompromising advocacy of Islamic purity that garnered him his initial following in Iran. In the 1950s, he was lauded as an ayatollah, a prominent religious figure. By the early 1960s, he had attained the title of grand ayatollah, therefore establishing himself as one of the most influential religious leaders among the Shiʿi community in Iran.

The White Revolution was an ambitious modernization programme that was initiated by the Shah in the early 1960s. This programme featured more liberation of women, less religious instruction, and a populist land reform legislation that disturbed the old nobility. The White Revolution was also known as the Shah's White Revolution. In particular, the implementation of these policies had the effect of diminishing and disenfranchising the powerful influence of the clerical class. However, it also had a wide-ranging impact on Iranian life and society. It had a negative impact on rural economies, it led to rapid urbanisation and Westernisation, it upended traditional social norms and values, and it prompted concerns about democracy and human rights. As a result, the resistance to the government brought together conservative clerics, the secular left, and other individuals, who often found a platform of agreement under the flag of Shi'i identity.

It was at this period that Khomeini became an outspoken opponent of the programme that the Shah was implementing. He also fueled antigovernment riots, which would ultimately result in his imprisonment in 1963. On November 4, 1964, Khomeini was transported out of Iran against his will after being imprisoned for a period of one year. In the end, he made his home in the city of Al-Najaf, which is considered to be Iraq's intellectual equivalent to Qom. There, he started the process of creating and spreading his ideas of velāyat-e faqīh, which translates to "guardianship of the jurist." These beliefs would ultimately serve as the basis for the establishment of an Islamic republic in Iran. He created a powerful and prominent network while he was living in exile, which put him in a position to play a leading role in the fall of the Shah. He also acquired a considerable following during his time in exile.

# 80.

# JAMES MADISON (USA)

One of the Founding Fathers of the United States and its fourth president (1809–1837), James Madison was born on March 16 (or March 5, Old Style) in 1751 in Port Conway, Virginia, United States, and died on June 28, 1836 in Montpelier, Virginia, United States. While in the Constitutional Convention (1787), he helped write and ratify the United States Constitution and published the Federalist papers with Alexander Hamilton and John Jay. The first ten amendments to the Constitution, often known as the Bill of Rights, were introduced by him when he was a member of the newly formed House of Representatives. When President Thomas Jefferson bought the Louisiana Territory from France, he was secretary of state. During his administration, the War of 1812 was fought.

James Madison: residence in historic Montpelier, Virginia

James Madison: residence in historic Montpelier, Virginia

Montpelier, Virginia, the residence of James Madison.

The house of Madison's maternal grandmother was the site of his birth. He lived his whole life in Virginia at Montpelier, close to the Blue Ridge Mountains. His father was a prominent landowner and squire in Orange County, and he was the son and heir apparent. Because of its anti-popery stance, he rode a horse to Princeton University, then known as the College of New Jersey, in 1769. He managed to finish the four-year programme in only two years, all while taking part in anti-English protests and ribaldly slamming a rival literary club. A combination of early advocacy of independence (1774) and fervent denunciation of the imprisonment of nearby Dissenters from the established Anglican church, as well as epilepsy and visions of early death brought on by years of overwork, prevented military training but did not prohibit home study of public law. Although Madison never joined a religion, he did say that Unitarianism was his favourite denomination when he was older.

Despite his worsening condition, he was elected to the Virginia Revolutionary Convention in 1776 and established the state's guarantee of religious freedom at that time. He assisted Thomas Jefferson in dismantling the church at the convention-turned-legislature, but he was unsuccessful in being re-elected because he refused to provide the electors with free whisky. March 1780 saw his transfer from the governor's council to the Continental Congress, after he had served there for two years.

His meek demeanour belied his forceful deeds; he waited six months before taking the stage, despite being five feet four inches tall, roughly 100 pounds, small-boned, boyish-looking, and having a weak voice. In the midst of a power struggle between proponents of state sovereignty and those who wanted the United States and France to work together in peace talks, he took the lead in demanding the Mississippi River be recognised as a western territorial border and the freedom to cross it via the Spanish-controlled delta. By convincing Virginia to relinquish the western lands to Congress as a national heritage, Madison was able to defeat the land speculators who were primarily interested in validating barrel-of-rum purchases from Indian tribes and denying Virginia's charter title to the expansive Northwest.

In 1781, after the Articles of Confederation were ratified, Madison set out to fortify the Union by using Congress's implicit authority to compel the states to pay for financial requisitions by military action.

After this failed, he tirelessly sought an amendment giving the authority to tax more money and penned a moving speech pleading with the states to accept the proposed article in order to save the country from collapsing. "Recognised as the man of the soundest judgement in Congress," wrote the French envoy to the US, the chevalier de la Luzerne, of Madison.

# 81.

# CHIANG KAI-SHEK (CHINA)

Chiang Kai-shek, a prominent figure in Chinese politics and the military, became a member of the Chinese Nationalist Party, sometimes referred to as the Kuomintang or KMT, in the year 1918. He succeeded Sun Yat-sen, the founder of the Kuomintang (KMT), as head of the party in 1925. He was responsible for the successful unification of China and the expulsion of Chinese communists from the party. In spite of the fact that Chiang's administration claimed to be focused on reform, its primary priority was on combating communism inside China as well as opposing Japanese invasion. China assumed its position as one of the Big Four nations when the Allies waged war on Japan in 1941. The year 1946 saw the beginning of a civil war, which ultimately resulted in the triumph of Mao Zedong's Communist troops and the establishment of the People's Republic of China. From 1949 until the time of his death, Chiang headed the KMT government in exile in Taiwan. This administration, which many nations continued to recognise as China's legitimate government, was still in power.

Chiang was born on October 31, 1887, in the coastal province of Chekiang. After his father passed away, Chiang fled his home and joined the army of the province. Initially, he attended the Paoting Military Academy in northern China, and then he went on to obtain his professional military training in Japan. In 1911, when uprisings against the Qing (Manchu) monarchy that was dominating China broke out, Chiang went home and joined the resistance. This struggle ultimately resulted in the destruction of the Manchus and the establishment of a Chinese republic. In 1918, he became a member of the Nationalist Party, which was established by Sun Yat-sen and was also referred to as the Kuomintang or KMT.

In 1924, Chiang established a military school in Whampoa, which is located close to Canton, with the assistance of Sun. In accordance with the strategies that Chiang had witnessed during his trip to the Soviet Union, he started the process of constructing the Nationalist army. During this same time period, Chinese Communists were allowed to join the KMT; but, following Sun's death in 1925, they started to come into conflict with factions of the party that were more conservative. In his role as Sun's successor, Chiang launched a successful military campaign against local warlords in northern China. Additionally, Chiang secured authority inside his own party by removing the Communists from power via a violent revolution in 1927. 1928 was the year when he established a new central government out of Nanking, and he appointed himself as the head of state.

# 82.

# OTTO I (HOLY ROMAN EMPIRE)

Westerners mourned the Roman Empire for centuries after Romulus Augustulus, the last emperor, was ousted in 476. The result was one of history's weirdest organisations. Voltaire mockingly said the Holy Roman Empire was neither holy nor Roman nor an empire. Despite subsequent events, Pope Leo III crowned Charlemagne, King of the Franks, Imperator Romanorum (Emperor of the Romans) at Rome in 800, leading the endeavour to establish a secular rule in Europe.

After Charlemagne's death in 814, the final Carolingian rulers ruled northern and central Italy. Berengar of Friuli, the last, was killed in 924. The title became more legitimate when it transferred to the East Frankish monarchs of Germany. Some German dukes elected Duke Henry the Fowler of Saxony king in 919 and kept the Magyars, Slavs, and Danes at bay. His powerful son Otto I, who succeeded him in 936, was more ambitious. He anointed himself king at Charlemagne's capital, Aachen. One account claims that the other German dukes served him at his crowning feast as vassals, indicating his imperial aspirations.

Otto was in his mid-20s. A fierce warrior and savvy politician, he destroyed all resistance, including two rebellions by his brother Henry, who meant to kill him. Otto wisely pardoned him and made him Duke of Bavaria when Henry was faithful. He also gave his family additional German dukedoms. He successfully manipulated French politics, repressed Bohemians, and encouraged German colonisation of Slavic area east of the Elbe and Oder. He defeated the Magyars of Hungary, pushed the Danes back in the north, made devoted friends of the German bishops (who he transformed into feudal lords and ecclesiastics), and founded a semi-German kingdom.

Otto invaded Italy in 951, when Berengar of Ivrea had usurped the throne and captured Adelaide, the former king's widow. She fled and sought German help when he forced her to marry his son. Otto conquered the Alps, became Lombard King, and married Adelaide. He let Berengar rule Italy as his vassal.

Pope John XII, noted for his drunkenness, required aid defeating Berengar, who had taken part of the Papal States, in 961. He appealed to Otto, who happily saved him and was proclaimed Roman Emperor by the pope. Otto conquered and imprisoned Berengar, but the pope became unhappy with Otto's supremacy and began manipulating him. Otto returned to Rome in 963 and ousted Pope John with an obedient synod of bishops. He replaced him with his preferred Roman, Pope Leo VIII.

Otto again interfered in Rome the next year when Pope Leo was overthrown and a new pope was appointed. The emperor ended that and returned to Rome to install his own nominee as Pope John XIII when Leo died in 965. Otto crushed an uprising against him. He took the papacy in a manner Pope John XII never planned.

Otto interfered in the eastern Roman Empire's realm in southern Italy, therefore the Byzantines accepted his imperial claim in 972. To marry his son and heir, Otto, they gave him Theophano, a Byzantine princess.

For two centuries, Otto the Great was not called Holy, yet historians consider him the first Holy Roman Emperor and the most powerful European monarch. He died in 973, leaving Otto II as his sole son.

It helped because Otto II had no brothers to challenge him, and the Ottonian dynasty lasted until 1024. The restored western Roman Empire became Holy in the 12th century and the German Nation's Holy Roman Empire in the early 1500s. After 1,000 years, Charlemagne's name was dropped in 1806.

# 83.

# FERDINAND MARCOS (PHILIPPINES)

Nationalist president Ferdinand Marcos (1917-1989) was a corrupt tyrant who imposed political persecution and brutality. He used charisma, fortune, political ties among Filipinos and Americans, military clout, and his wife, former beauty pageant queen Imelda Marcos, to become president.

Marcos, an Aglipayan Catholic and subsequently a Roman Catholic, claimed to have supernatural visions to govern the Philippines. He also referenced Philippine Adam and Eve by calling himself malakas (strong) and Imelda maganda (beautiful). He used the Catholic Church to achieve his political goals and gain public support. However, the Catholic Church mobilised the bulk of the populace in a People Power display, defeating him.

Marcos was specifically criticised for the $50 million USD campaign spending that devalued the Philippine peso by 50% by his second term. Security forces brutally quashed leftist and student demonstrations. Marcos accused numerous Catholic priests, who were now publicly criticising him, of inciting demonstrations. Marcos enjoyed support from family, politics, and the US government, which provided more military help to fight communism.

Marcos declared martial rule before the 1973 elections, ending his two presidential mandates but intending to serve as Prime Minister under a new legislative system. He surreptitiously orchestrated public violence to legitimise martial rule and imprison his opponents, including opposition leader Benigno Aquino Jr., leftist activists, intellectuals, journalists, priests and nuns, and students. He called for a constitutional conference and paid political figures to prolong his presidency and establish a parliament. In opposition to Marcos, various leftist organisations formed under the National Democratic Front. Priests and nuns who joined communist Christians for National Liberation were jailed and tortured.

After Benigno Aquino Jr. was assassinated, the Church supported his widow Corazon for presidency. Marcos requested early presidential elections in 1986, believing he could win rigged elections again. The Church funded volunteers to watch the vote, and he seemed to capture the presidency again until thirty state-run Commission on Elections (COMELEC) staffers left, charging electoral fraud, and were hidden by the Church. After COMELEC reported the result, the Church called it illegitimate and issued a formal announcement stating Corazon Aquino had won, sparking large demonstrations. Along with hundreds of others, kneeling nuns said the rosary outside the military facility where Marcos defectors were imprisoned in a People Power demonstration.

Marcos was evacuated to Guam by American helicopters on February 25, 1986, and ultimately to Hawaii, where he died in 1989. His wife Imelda and others have become elected leaders in the Philippines.

# 84.

# BORIS YELTSIN (RUSSIA)

Boris Yeltsin was a Russian politician who emerged as the President of Russia in the year 1990. He was born on February 1, 1931 in Sverdlovsk, which is now known as Yekaterinburg, Russia, Soviet Union, and passed away on April 23, 2007, in Moscow, Russia. In 1991, he became the first leader in the history of the country to be chosen by the people. He led Russia through a turbulent decade of political and economic retrenchment until his departure on the eve of the year 2000. Yeltsin joined the Communist Party in 1961 after attending the Urals Polytechnic Institute and working on a variety of construction projects in the Sverdlovsk oblast between the years 1955 and 1968 on his way to becoming a member of the party. After beginning his full-time employment with the party in 1968, he was promoted to the position of first secretary of the Sverdlovsk oblast party committee in 1976. Following that, he became acquainted with Mikhail Gorbachev, who was serving as his equivalent in the city of Stavropol at the time. After Gorbachev came to power, he selected Yeltsin in 1985 to clear up the corruption in the Moscow party organisation. In 1986, he raised Yeltsin to the Politburo (as a nonvoting member), marking the beginning of his tenure as leader of the party. When Yeltsin began criticising the slow pace of reform at party meetings, challenging party conservatives, as well as criticising Gorbachev himself, he alienated Gorbachev. Yeltsin was able to demonstrate that he was a capable and determined reformer while serving as the mayor of Moscow, which meant that he was the first secretary of Moscow's Communist Party committee. Yeltsin was compelled to retire from the leadership of the Moscow party in 1987 and from the Politburo in 1988. He did so in a state of widespread shame.

## 85.

# GUSTAVUS ADOLPHUS (SWEDEN)

He was the King of Sweden from 1611 until 1632, Gustavus Adolphus, who was born on December 9, 1594 in Stockholm, Sweden, and died on November 6, 1632 in Lutzen, Saxony, which is today in Germany. He was the one who established the foundations of the modern Swedish state and made Sweden a prominent power in Europe.

He was the oldest son of Charles IX and Christina of Holstein, who was his second wife. Gustavus was the eldest son. He was just a few weeks away from becoming 17 years old when he succeeded his father in 1611, and the Swedish Estates (the Riksdag, or Assembly) only let him to take full control of the government in return for significant constitutional concessions. He was only a few weeks away from his 17th birthday. It turned out that he was in a situation that was quite challenging for him. Charles IX had taken the throne by removing his nephew Sigismund III Vasa, who was also the king of Poland, from his position in 1599. As a consequence of this dynastic dispute, Sweden and Poland were embroiled in a conflict that lasted intermittently for sixty years. Both the possibility of a legitimist invasion from Poland and the effort to restore the older Vasa line were always something that Gustavus had to take into consideration up to the year 1629. There was also a war that Charles had started in Russia in an effort to push up his younger son, Charles Philip, for the vacant Russian throne. After that, when his soldiers were severely invested in Russia, he had rashly initiated a war with Denmark. In addition to putting Sweden in a precarious position on the international stage, Charles had also left behind a legacy of internal problems for the country to deal with. After his usurpation of the throne, not only did it result in the expulsion of a Roman Catholic sovereign whose rule appeared to threaten Sweden's Lutheranism, but it also resulted in the defeat of the aristocratic constitutionalism of the Council of State. Furthermore, it was followed by the execution of five prominent members of the high aristocracy. As a result of his theological beliefs (he was accused of leaning towards Calvinism), Charles had been embroiled in an ongoing conflict with the Lutheran church. His reign had been arbitrary and brutal. The kingdom was tired by incessant conflict at the time of his death, the monarchy was largely unpopular, & the accession of a new king seemed to give the chance to demand assurances from the crown against a return of misgovernment being imposed on the country.

# 86.

# SADDAM HUSSEIN (IRAQ)

President Saddam Hussein (1979-2003) was a harsh dictator who waged expensive and futile wars against surrounding nations.

Saddam took over the government in 1979 and became president when Bakr resigned. He became prime minister, Revolutionary Command Council chairman, and more. He utilised a large secret police force to repress internal resistance to his reign and created a personality cult in Iraq. His aims as president were to replace Egypt as Arab international leader and dominate the Persian Gulf.

In September 1980, Saddam invaded Iran's oil resources, but the conflict was attritional. Saddam cut his economic growth plans due to the war's expense and oil export disruption. Iran and Iraq reached a cease-fire in 1988, ending the war. Saddam built increased his army despite Iraq's massive foreign debt after the war.

Iraq conquered Kuwait in August 1990. Saddam wanted to utilise Kuwait's massive oil profits to boost Iraq's economy, but his takeover of Kuwait immediately sparked a global trade boycott. Despite the growth of a strong U.S.-led military presence in Saudi Arabia and UN resolutions denouncing the occupation and authorising action to end it, he refused to remove his men from Kuwait. The international military coalition expelled Iraqi forces from Kuwait six weeks after the Persian Gulf War started on January 16, 1991. After Iraq's defeat, Shiʿis and Kurds rebelled, but Saddam crushed them, leading to thousands fleeing to refugee camps along the northern border. Many thousands more were tortured and killed, vanishing into government jails like Abu Ghraib.

The UN cease-fire agreement prevented Iraq from creating or possessing chemical, biological, and nuclear weapons. Many sanctions were imposed on the nation awaiting compliance, disrupting the economy. The US and UK launched Operation Desert Fox, a four-day air campaign, in late 1998 because Saddam refused to cooperate with UN weapons inspectors. Both nations pledged to help the Iraqi opposition overthrow Saddam, whose administration had become more ruthless under UN sanctions, but the Iraqi leader banned UN weapons inspectors from entering his country. It became evident that Saddam was preparing one of his sons, Uday or Qusay, to replace him. Both rose to power and resembled their father's harshness. Saddam also strengthened his grip at home while voicing defiance and anti-Americanism. Even though he was increasingly feared at home, Saddam was seen as the only Arab leader ready to oppose American assault.

After the 2001 September 11 attacks, the U.S. administration renewed the disarmament process, fearing Saddam might provide terrorists with chemical or biological weapons. In November 2002, Saddam permitted UN weapons inspectors to return to Iraq, but his refusal to comply upset the US and UK, who ended talks. On March 17, 2003, U.S. President George W. Bush urged Saddam to resign and leave Iraq within 48 hours or face war. He also said that U.S. troops could be required to stabilise the new administration and seek for WMDs. On March 20, U.S. and ally troops attacked Iraq after Saddam refused to quit.

The Iraq War began with U.S. jets attacking a bunker complex where Saddam was meeting with subordinates. The strike failed to kill Saddam, but following attacks made it apparent that removing him was a primary invasion aim. Saddam, ever stubborn, urged Iraqis to die to oppose U.S. and British troops, but resistance faltered, and on April 9, when Baghdad fell to U.S. forces, Saddam escaped into hiding. He fled with much of the national treasure before U.S. soldiers caught him. After his sons Uday and Qusay were trapped and murdered in Mosul on July 22, Saddam was seized on December 13. The once-dapper commander was found unclean and dishevelled in an underground hiding hole in a farmhouse near Tikrīt. Although armed, Saddam surrendered to U.S. forces without fire.

# 87.

# LECH WAŁĘSA (POLAND)

In Popowo, Poland, Lech Walesa was born on September 29, 1943. A machine centre employed him as a vehicle mechanic from 1961 to 1965 after he graduated from vocational school. at 1967, he became an electrician at the Gdansk shipyards after two years in the army as a corporal. He married Danuta Golos in 1969 and has eight children.

He was one of the shipyard workers' leaders during the December 1970 government-worker conflict and temporarily arrested. However, his shop stewardship got him dismissed in 1976, forcing him to work interim jobs.

He and other activists formed free non-communist trade unions in 1978 and participated in various seacoast protests. State security monitoring and detentions plagued him.

Walesa led the Gdansk shipyard strike in August 1980, which sparked nationwide strikes. The main demands were worker rights. The authorities were compelled to negotiate with Walesa the Gdansk Agreement on August 31, 1980, which allowed workers to strike and form their own union.

Catholics backed the movement, and Pope John Paul II welcomed Walesa to the Vatican in January 1981. Walesa always looked to his Catholicism for strength and inspiration. The International Labour Organisation hosted Walesa in Italy, Japan, Sweden, France, and Switzerland in 1980–81. He was elected Solidarity Chairman at the First National Solidarity Congress in Gdansk in September 1981.

After a short period of relative freedom, General Jaruzelski established martial rule, "suspended" Solidarity, imprisoned several of its leaders, and jailed Walesa in a distant rural residence in December 1981, fearing Soviet military invasion.

Walesa returned to the Gdansk shipyards in November 1982. Despite being monitored, he remained in touch with underground Solidarity leaders. Many civil code limitations remained after martial control was abolished in July 1983. The underground movement cheered Walesa's Nobel Award in October 1983, while the official press criticised it.

The Jaruzelski dictatorship had to negotiate with Walesa and Solidarity when economic circumstances deteriorated and it became even more unpopular. The outcome was restricted parliamentary elections that established a non-communist administration. The Soviet Union no longer used military force to maintain communist parties in satellite governments after Mikhail Gorbachev.

Walesa started interacting with international leaders as chairman of the resurrected Solidarity union.

Solidarity's second national congress elected Walesa chairperson with 77.5% of the vote in April 1990. In December 1990, a national election elected him Polish president. His November 1995 election loss ended his tenure.

Walesa has multiple honorary degrees, notably from Harvard and Paris. Other awards include the Medal of Freedom (Philadelphia, U.S.), Award of Free World (Norway), and European Award of Human Rights.

# 88.

# OLIVER CROMWELL (UK)

William Steward's daughter Elizabeth and Robert Cromwell had Oliver Cromwell on April 25, 1599, at Huntingdon, a small village near Cambridge.

Morgan Williams, Oliver Cromwell's great-great-grandfather, married Katherine in 1497. Katherine was the sister of Henry VIII's senior minister Thomas Cromwell, who was raised to the earldom of Essex but killed in 1540.

Morgan and Katherine's three kids named themselves Cromwell after their renowned maternal uncle. Several of their descendants utilised Williams-alias-Cromwell. Some family members briefly changed their surname to Williams during the Restoration to dissociate themselves from Oliver Cromwell.

Richard, Morgan Williams and Katherine Cromwell's oldest son, had two Cromwell sons, Henry and Francis. Henry was knighted like his father, and Robert, Oliver's father, was the youngest of his eleven children by his first marriage.

Cromwell's humble origins and early family life are not thoroughly chronicled, unlike his military and political career. For forty years, Cromwell was unknown, saying in 1654 that he was "by birth a gentleman, living neither in considerable height, nor yet in obscurity". The English civil wars of the 1640s gave him the chance to climb to prominence.

WWPDH Elizabeth BourchierAfter his father's modest inheritance, Cromwell became a minor landowner, farming and collecting tenancy rents. He was educated at Huntingdon Grammar School (now the Cromwell Museum) and the puritan-influenced Sidney Sussex College, Cambridge, run by the famous Calvinist Samuel Ward.

After Robert died in June 1617, Cromwell left Cambridge without a degree to assist his mother and seven unmarried sisters at home. While managing his father's land, Cromwell briefly studied law at Lincoln's Inn of Court in London, where he met his wife Elizabeth, daughter of Sir James Bourchier, a knighted London merchant and landowner with strong ties to Essex's puritan gentlemen.

Cromwell maintained his wife and growing family on his little wage (Oliver and Elizabeth had nine children, but only six survived maturity). Cromwell, the only son, supported his widowed mother, who outlived her husband by 37 years.

He moved to St Ives, Cambridgeshire, in 1631 and subsequently to Ely in 1636 after inheriting land from his maternal uncle. The inheritance's position and Cromwell's self-proclaimed 'spiritual awakening' in the 1630s led to a puritan lifestyle amid England's acute political and religious upheaval. Cromwell was a Cambridge MP but not active in national politics until the 1640s.

# 89.

# LEE KUAN YEW (SINGAPORE)

Politician and lawyer Lee Kuan Yew (born September 16, 1923, Singapore—died March 23, 2015, Singapore) was Singapore's prime minister from 1959 to 1990 Over his reign, Singapore became Southeast Asia's most wealthy nation.

Since the 19th century, Lee's family was Chinese in Singapore. First language was English; learned Chinese, Malay, and Tamil after joining politics. After studying in Singapore, Lee temporarily attended the London School of Economics and Political Science before graduating from Fitzwilliam House, Cambridge: law (1949). He topped the accolades list. He turned socialist. He returned to Singapore after being admitted to the English bar in 1950. He negotiated increased salaries for postal workers as the Postal Union's legal counsel and for other labour unions.

Singapore, a British crown colony and East Asia's main naval base, was administered by a governor and legislative council. Wealthy Chinese merchants were appointed to the council rather than elected.

Lee joined forces with lawyer David Saul Marshall and trade unionist Lim Yew Hock to fight the businesspeople on the council during constitutional change in Singapore in the early 1950s. Lee left his two colleagues to become secretary-general of his own party, the People's Action Party, and pursue a more extreme stance. The party contained communists, with Lee accepting sponsorship for years.

In 1955, a new constitution boosted council elected seats to 25 of 32. The Labour Front, created by Lee's old comrades, won 13 seats, while the PAP won 3—one of which Lee won for an area with many impoverished Chinese in Singapore.

The next year, Lee went to London as part of a Singaporean team that failed to seize independence. Many PAP leaders were imprisoned during Singaporean unrest. London discussions continued in 1957 with Lee on the delegation. Lee won an overwhelming by-election in Singapore after self-government was agreed upon. After a short power struggle within the PAP, Lee was deposed as secretary-general by the left wing in August but reappointed in October.

Lee negotiated Singapore's Commonwealth self-government status in London the following year (1958). The May 1959 elections under Singapore's new constitution saw Lee fight for social reforms and unification with Malaya on an anticolonialist, anticommunist platform. Lee's party won 43 of 51 seats, but he refused to form a government unless the British released his left-wing members imprisoned in 1956. After their release, Lee became prime minister on June 5, 1959, and established a government. His five-year plan included slum eradication, public housing construction, women's liberation, educational growth, and industrialization. Lee severed his links with the communists when the PAP's left-wing departed to create the Barisan Sosialis ("Socialist Front") in 1961. Lee and other PAP moderates dominated Singaporean politics thereafter.

# 90.

# JOSIP BROZ TITO (YUGOSLAVIA)

Josip Tito (1892-1980), a Croatian soldier and socialist revolutionary, ruled Yugoslavia authoritarianly throughout the Cold War. The peasant farmer's 15 children included Josip Broz, born near the Croatian-Slovenian border. Locksmith-trained Broz left home to work in Zagreb. He joined the Austro-Hungarian army and fought on the Russian front during World War I. Broz became a sergeant-major in his early 20s after impressive military service. He became a Russian prisoner of war in Galicia in 1915. He attended the October Revolution in Petrograd after his 1917 release. Broz supported Vladimir Lenin and operated in communist-held areas during the Russian Civil War (1918-20). He returned to Yugoslavia in 1920.

Once home, Broz was a waiter. He joined the modest but illegal Yugoslav Communist Party and the union movement. He was imprisoned for five years for political actions in 1928. Broz became Tito and lived underground after his release. He joined the Communist Party Central Committee in 1934 and became leader three years later. Tito became resistance leader in 1941 when the Nazis invaded Yugoslavia. Tito looked a natural leader for post-war Yugoslavia after his wartime success. He became prime minister in November 1944 while directing the resistance. Elections in November 1945 reaffirmed Tito's power. He established the Federal People's Republic of Yugoslavia and a republican constitution in January 1946.

At first, the world saw Tito as another Moscow servant, submissive to Stalin. However, the Yugoslavs had emancipated themselves without Soviet support, and Tito was no puppet. Belgrade and Moscow immediately disagreed on economic growth. Tito resisted Stalin by creating syndicalist socialism that gave workers more control over production. After Soviet efforts to overthrow Tito failed, Yugoslavia withdrew from the Cominform in 1949, provoking border force mobilisations and invasion concerns. Stalin reportedly ordered three assassination attempts on Tito, who famously replied, "Stop sending people to kill me. We have caught five of them. If you keep sending murderers, I'll send one to Moscow and not send another. The Soviet-Yugoslav split enabled Tito to seek US help. President Harry Truman approved this help in 1951.

Moscow and Belgrade relations thawed after Stalin's 1953 death. Independent and unpredictable, Tito never committed to an alliance. He promoted "positive neutralism" in foreign policy, engaging with the Soviet bloc and Western countries. Tito arrested political opponents, alleged Soviet sympathisers, and critics at home. His administration had a secret police and political prisoner work camps like Goli Otok. Socialist Federal Republic of Yugoslavia was established in 1963. Despite its socialist stance Religious liberties and private capital ownership were permitted under Tito. To network with socialist and democratic leaders, Tito travelled the globe. He hosted the 1961 founding of the Non-Aligned Movement (NAM), a coalition of Cold War leaders outside of the Soviet and Western blocs.

Tito initiated or authorised political changes in the early 1970s to liberalise Yugoslavia and give regions more autonomy. New federal constitution enacted in 1974. Tito's health and influence deteriorated. The 85-year-old Yugoslavian leader toured the Soviet Union, China, and North Korea in 1978. In May 1980, Tito died. Due to the 1970s reforms and the loss of this uniting leader, Yugoslavia broke apart and fought in the Balkans.

# 91.

# KING LOUIS XVI (FRANCE)

Louis XVI, the final Ancien Regime French monarch, was born on August 23, 1754. Third son of the dauphin or heir. Louis became dauphin and heir after his father's death. As the heir, Louis was encouraged to hide his genuine sentiments, which caused historians to debate his intellect. He knew English and Latin well, loved history and geography, and had a good recall. In the pivotal moments that led to the French Revolution, he was noted for his character weakness and political inexperience.

Louis married Marie-Antoinette, the daughter of Austrian empress Maria-Theresa and Holy Roman Emperor Francis I, in 1770 to strengthen France-Austria relations. After his grandfather Louis XV died four years later, Louis became King of France and Navarre. Although immature and self-conscious, the young king cared about his countrymen and wanted to improve French foreign policy.

His main foreign policy goal was to promote the American Revolution to avenge Great Britain and restore France's dominance in Europe.

French cooperation helped the Americans succeed, but funding the effort drove the already-failing French government to bankruptcy. His wife was also accused of living lavishly on French gold. A French food scarcity exacerbated the king's problems.

In 1787, Louis backed dramatic fiscal, economic, and administrative changes recommended by his ministers to save the sinking French ship, but conservatives opposed them. In July 1788, Louis called the Estates-General for the first time since 1614. Three primary "estates" of French society—nobles, clergy, and commoners—formed the Estates-General parliament. After the Estates-General rejected numerous reform proposals, the Third Estate (the largest) declared themselves the National Assembly and pressed forward with reforms without the First or Second Estates' consent, distracted by his son's death in June 1789 and a refusal to work with royally titled estates.

Louis signed the death sentence for historic French feudalism by accepting the National Assembly's power. Louis outwardly accepted his new status as a constitutional king, although privately believing the revolution would end and restore the monarchy. His popularity increased once he visited Paris instead of Versailles. He was termed a "restorer of French liberty."

He promptly opposed the National Assembly's demands. at response, a crowd of enraged Parisian women dragged the king and his family from Versailles to Paris, where they were imprisoned at the Tuileries Palace. In disguise as servants, Louis and his family tried to flee to Austria on June 21, 1791. Their capture at Varennes led them back to Paris under surveillance. This act severely tarnished Louis's constitutional monarchy and alienated the public.

Foreign involvement was Louis and Marie-Antoinette's final chance. Louis advised the National Assembly to go to war with Austria because he believed the French revolutionary troops would be destroyed and his power restored. He subsequently rejected a new constitution, choosing deceit and trickery under his wife's influence. War broke out in April 1792 when the Duke of Brunswick promised to destroy Paris if the royal family was endangered again. A second Parisian mob took the Tuileries Palace. The First French Republic was declared on September 22, 1792, overthrowing the monarchy after repeated military losses and civil discontent.

The National Convention, the First Republic's legislative body, tried Louis for treason after discovering his counterrevolutionary actions at the Tuileries Palace. Louis, as Citizen Capet, appeared twice before the Convention but was convicted of treason and executed on January 18, 1793. The former monarch was carried to the guillotine in the Place de la Revolution (now the Place de la Concorde) and killed on January 21 with dignity. Nine months later, his wife died. Louis's irresolution, lack of political understanding, and foreign policy mistakes expedited the French Revolution, but it would have needed a strong and steady hand to avert the Ancien Regime's demise.

# 92.

# HAILE SELASSIE (ETHIOPIA)

Ethiopian monarch from 1930 to 1974, Haile Selassie I (born July 23, 1892, near Harer, Ethiopia—died August 27, 1975, Addis Ababa), modernised his nation and led it into post-World War II African politics. He got Ethiopia into the League of Nations and UN and made Addis Ababa the OAU's main hub.

Tafari was the son of Emperor Menilek II's main advisor Ras (Prince) Makonnen and a great-grandson of Sahle Selassie of Shewa (Shoa). Tafari was elevated after impressing the emperor with his intelligence while being educated at home by French missionaries. As governor of Sidamo and subsequently Harer province, he pursued progressive measures to shatter the feudal control of the local aristocracy by strengthening the central government with a paid civil service. Thus, he represented politically progressive people. He married Menilek II's great-granddaughter Wayzaro Menen in 1911.

After Menilek II died in 1913, his grandson Lij Yasu took the king, but the majority Christian Ethiopians disliked him due to his unreliability and Islamism. Tafari led the Christian rebellion and toppled Lij Yasu in 1916. In 1917, Menilek II's daughter Zauditu became empress, and Ras Tafari became regent and heir presumptive.

Zauditu was traditional, while Ras Tafari was progressive and inspired modernist youth. He successfully admitted Ethiopia to the League of Nations in 1923. He became the first Ethiopian king to visit Jerusalem, Rome, Paris, and London the following year. He became negus ("king") in 1928 and emperor (November 2, 1930) after Zauditu died. He was christened Haile Selassie ("Might of the Trinity"). He issued a new constitution in 1931 that severely curtailed Parliament. As Ethiopia's government from the late 1920s, Haile Selassie established regional schools, strengthened the police, and outlawed feudal taxes to benefit his people and strengthen the central government.

After Italy invaded Ethiopia in 1935, Haile Selassie headed the fight, but he was exiled in May 1936. He gave a famous statement to the League of Nations in Geneva on June 30, 1936, requesting assistance. He formed an Ethiopian exile army in Sudan with British help during World War II. British and Ethiopian armies invaded Ethiopia in January 1941 and retook Addis Ababa months later. After being reinstalled as emperor, Haile Selassie had to regain his power. He again implemented social, economic, & educational reforms to slowly modernise Ethiopian government and society.

Haile Selassie's personal influence dominated the Ethiopian administration. He handed himself equal authority in 1955 with a new constitution. A dissident branch of the army took control of Addis Ababa in December 1960 and was overthrown by loyalists after a fierce battle.

In 1963, Haile Selassie helped establish the Organisation of African Unity. Famine, rising unemployment, and political stagnation caused army revolt in 1974, ending his authority in Ethiopia. The Derg, a Marxist military regime, replaced Haile Selassie. Haile Selassie spent his life under house imprisonment in his castle. His death was first ascribed to natural reasons, but subsequent evidence suggested he was strangled by the military administration.

# 93.

# PETER THE GREAT (RUSSIA)

Peter I (Peter the Great) was Tsar of Russia from 1682-1721 and Emperor from 1721-1725. Peter held absolute control throughout his long reign and built Russia's first navy, industrialised, established educational institutions, and founded St. Petersburg.

With his long travel to Western Europe (the Grand Embassy), Peter adored learning from strangers. This tour helped him modernise Russia and put it on par with other great European nations.

Peter was born in Moscow (May 30, 1672). He was born to Tsar Alexis (1629-1676) & his second wife Natalya Kirillovna Naryshkina (1651-1694). Although he was Tsar Alexis' third son, his birth was celebrated since his older half-brothers, Feodor (1661-1682) & Ivan (1666-1696), were unwell and weak. Due to his healthy birth, the Tsaritsa family was honoured and promoted. Peter was christened on June 29, Saint Peter's feast day in the Russian Orthodox Church.

Peter was raised in luxury by a governess, a wet nurse, and a staff of playmates and friends who followed his every wish. Nikita Zotov (1644-1717) taught Peter Russian history epics. Peter became longtime friends with Zotov and vowed to restore Russia to its former splendour if he became tsar.

Peter could remarry after divorcing Eudoxia in 1698. He married Lithuanian peasant Marta Skavronskaya (later Catherine I of Russia, l. 1684-1727). Peter saw her working in Prince Menshikov's (1673-1729) home and was immediately drawn to her. She joined Peter's domestic servant and married secretly in 1707, making their marriage official in 1712.

They had twelve children, but only Anna (1708-1728) and Elizabeth (1709-1762) survived adulthood. Catherine became emperor after Peter died without heirs.

In his final weeks, Peter the Great was unwell and died on January 28, 1725. Some criticise his dictatorial rule, while others regard it as a golden age for Russia. Peter was dedicated to helping Russia. He immediately pursued fresh chances he believed would benefit Russia. Although some may find his actions hazardous, it is noteworthy that he personally participated in every new venture rather than directing others to do likewise. His legacy lives on in St. Petersburg and his educational institutes.

# 94.

# EMPEROR TIBERIUS (ROME)

To be anticipated, considering that he was just the second Roman Emperor and the heir of the deified Augustus, Tiberius Claudius Caesar is one of the more famous but still contentious Caesars. According to Father Reginald Foster, a papal Latinist, he was undeniably "a hard man" and was seen by some as a brutal dictator. He was a complex, multi-faceted, and ever-changing personality, much like many historical emperors, but notably the Romans. His abilities as a commander and, subsequently, a leader, were undeniable. But much of the nitpicking about him is based on his last years, when he seemed to descend into madness and paranoia. But it's important to keep in mind that, like with many Roman emperors, our evaluation of these men is heavily reliant on the writings of others, and that these writers were frequently political opponents who may have embellished the truth in order to paint their subjects in the worst possible light. On the other hand, Christians remember him as the Roman Emperor who ruled throughout the ministry of Christ, and he is important to the world as the successor of Augustus. Emperor Tiberius was the Caesar

Jesus meant when he stated, "Render unto Caesar..." on a number of occasions.

His namesake Tiberius Claudius Nero was born to Livia Drusilla, who subsequently divorced his father and married the Emperor Augustus in 39 BC. The birth took place on November 16, 42 BC. Augustus adopted Tiberius as his son and successor, and he became known as Tiberius Julius Caesar after marrying his step-sister Julia the Elder. Nevertheless, Tiberius was not a power-hungry ambitious guy, even with these illustrious family ties. With a modest understanding of the world and its harsh facts, he lacked an idealised view of power and understood that its potential benefits were accompanied with just as large, if not greater, risks. He was a serious king who felt the full force of his power and responsibilities; he became a hermit and, as his paranoia worsened, a terrifying figure whom his subjects drew terror from instead of admiration. Many Romans were elated when he died, but many may have come to regret their judgements of Tiberius and their joy at his passing when they considered that his adoptive grandson Caligula replaced him.

Although Emperor Augustus elevated him to high administrative positions in an effort to groom him for the throne, he secretly wished for an heir from his own family. Tiberius was a very effective commander who achieved many wins throughout his time spent battling on the Roman borders. Not only did he overcome the Parthians in Armenia, but he also wed Marcus Agrippa's daughter, battled the Galls and the Germans, encountered barbarians in the French Alps, and discovered the Danube's source. In 13 BC, he returned to Rome to become consul and welcome his first son, Julius Caesar Drusus. Tiberius and Drusus rose through the ranks after the death of General Agrippa in 12 BC, which shocked Rome. Fantastic, isn't it? Seems like Tiberius isn't impressed. One of the most "horizontally accessible" women in the Roman Empire was his step-sister Julia the Elder, whom Emperor Augustus had him marry after divorcing his wife. Indeed, it should come as no surprise that Tiberius began to equate personal anguish and suffering with power and reputation.

Reportedly, Augustus was forced to choose Tiberius as his successor despite his reluctance, due to matters of state. Following the demise of the other possible successors, Tiberius became "the only game in town," despite his initial impression that he was too severe and intimidating. When Augustus died and Tiberius became Emperor in 14 AD, he had a stellar record in the military but was unprepared for the role of administrator. It was a bit of a monkey wrench, but this was the first time Rome's authority had ever been passed down through the generations in this way. The Senate had to choose his successor Augustus and deal with challengers; in other instances, the legions rebelled and had to be crushed. Germanicus, Tiberius's adoptive son, was sent to deal with this and then led the border troops forward into Germany. Tiberius summoned Germanicus back from his conquests and put an end to their growth; upon his return, he was still greeted with victory. After the death of the well-liked Germanicus, several people accused Tiberius of being involved.

The Dowager Empress Livia, his mother, was a major source of stress for him. In an effort to escape her, he once departed Rome for his island castle of Capri. He withdrew from the endeavour to deify her, skipped her burial, and flat-out rejected her will when she passed away. Sejanus, who had essentially become Tiberius' right-hand man after he had left Rome for his pleasure grotto on Capri, suspected Agrippina and her son Nero of conspiring against him, so he imprisoned them in 29 AD. Naevius Sutorius Macro succeeded Sejanus, who had been assassinated for supposedly conspiring against Tiberius, and the air was thick with conspiracy theories. At Tiberius' death, he would play a contentious role in the succession to the throne and remain an important figure during the remainder of his reign. But I'm straying from the point.

The fact that Tiberius was a successful emperor is easy to overlook. When he first came to power, he did his utmost to emulate Augustus. He presided over the senate with diligence, went to athletic events, distributed presents, and sometimes contributed generously. He was very dedicated to his work, yet he was socially awkward compared to his stepfather. His demeanour was often cold, haughty, and intolerable. After slashing funding for public entertainment as part of his austerity measures, he became fairly unpopular. Even though they had food, the Romans felt tricked by the circus. Even while he had ultimate say over matters of governance, he mostly stood aside and let the provinces run their own shows. Unfortunately, he was unable to forge a friendship with the senators and eventually began to see the majority of them as possible adversaries.

Fearing plots against him at every turn, he retired into seclusion on Capri and had further senators and others executed, further increasing his unpopularity. Although his accounts of his actions on Capri are exaggerated, it is safe to say that he was in a poor state of mind as he neared the end of his life and had few prospects for the future. His adopted grandson Caligula had a reputation for frightening people from an early age, and his grandson Gemellus was too young to inherit anything. While his tax hikes did improve Rome's finances, they also enraged the population and earned him the senate's loathing and, likely, the conspiracy theories that led to his purportedly unnatural death on March 16, 37 AD (Macro was suspected of smothering him). Many Romans applauded and yelled "to the Tiber with Tiberius!" upon hearing of his death. The army had to discreetly cremate his remains away from public view after transporting him to Rome under heavy guard.

Although he was not publicly denounced, Emperor Tiberius was neither deified nor criticised, unlike Augustus. He had successfully ruled despite his widespread disapproval. During his 23 years as king, nothing terrible happened, and on the whole, he appears to have been a decent ruler—he was just unpopular. After he died and Caligula became emperor, one has to ask if his detractors began to miss him. Tiberius supposedly referred to his successor as "nursing a viper in the bosom of Rome" when he talked about him. When he took office, he said that he would measure his success by his ability to rule effectively and to do the right thing, regardless of public opinion. That is one area where history has mostly backed him up, even if the Romans would have to wait a long to realise it.

# 95.

# HUGO CHAVEZ (VENEZUELA)

Born on July 28, 1954, in Sabaneta, Barinas, Venezuela, Hugo Chávez was a politician and president of Venezuela from 1999 to 2013. He died on March 5, 2013, in Caracas. The "Bolivarian Revolution" was a socialist political programme that Chávez claimed to be spearheading throughout Latin America. It was named after the South American independence hero Simón Bolívar. A powerful military actively participating in public initiatives, nationalism, and a centrally planned economy are the essential components of the revolution, however their emphasis has shifted depending on Chávez's objectives. Many people came to recognise his philosophy as chavismo.

Sabaneta is a tiny village in Venezuela's southern lowlands where Chávez spent his childhood. Out of the six children that made it to adulthood, he was the only male. Hugo was brought up in the city of Barinas by his grandmother, Rosa Inés Chávez, who inculcated in him a passion for politics and history, since his parents, who were both teachers, could not afford to maintain all of their children. Hugo's older brother, Adán, was reared by their other grandmother.

During his adolescent years, Chávez was greatly impacted by the teachings of Bolívar and Karl Marx, the German philosopher and one of the founders of communism. These ideas had a tremendous effect on Chávez's political philosophy, which he received from José Esteban Ruiz Guevara, a local historian. Another factor that had a significant impact on Chávez was the existence of the National Liberation Armed Forces (Fuerzas Armadas de Liberación Nacional; FALN), a communist guerilla movement that started battling the Venezuelan government in the 1960s. Cuban leader Fidel Castro, who would subsequently become Chávez's political inspiration, backed the FALN.

Chávez enrolled at the Venezuelan Military college in 1971 in Caracas, the capital of Venezuela, not because he aspired to join the military but because the college had excellent baseball instructors, and he wanted to pursue his ambition of playing professional baseball. Chávez had intended to register, do well on the baseball team, and then leave. Even though he had great left-handed pitching skills, he was never going to make it as a professional, so he went back to school. But he was an ill-behaved and impoverished student who finished 1975 near the graduation ranks.

Second lieutenant was Chávez's military rank when he entered the service. Securing the surviving guerillas aligned with the left was his first mission. However, Chávez developed compassion for the rebels as he pursued them, seeing them as commoners struggling for liberation. After learning that his brother Adán had been covertly collaborating with the rebels in 1977, Chávez was prepared to leave the army out of anger. Douglas Bravo, a former FALN commander and current head of the clandestine Venezuelan Revolution Party (PRV), was someone Chávez set up to see. It was Bravo who "inspired me and I realised I wouldn't be leaving the army," Chávez said, years later. To internalise the revolutionary ideas of the rebels, Chávez and other military commanders clandestinely established the Bolivarian Movement 200 in 1982. A civilian-military coup d'état was their intended method of seizing power.

# 96.

# MANUEL NORIEGA (PANAMA)

Born on February 11, 1938, in Panama City, Panama, Manuel Noriega was a military leader and commander of the Panamanian Defence Forces from 1983 to 1989. During his time in office, he was the real power behind the civilian president. Noriega died on May 29, 2017, in Panama City.

Manuel Noriega (centre) is escorted by U.S. Drug Enforcement Administration officers to an aeroplane departing for the US on January 3, 1990.

A impoverished family of Colombian descent was Noriega's family. He attended a prestigious secondary school in Panama and then received a full scholarship to attend Lima's Chorrillos Military School. He got acquainted with Captain Omar Torrijos and progressed through the ranks after being commissioned a sublieutenant in the National Guard upon his return to Panama and stationed in Colón. In the military coup that deposed Arnulfo Arias's administration and allowed Torrijos to take power, Noriega was a participant. A subsequent coup attempt to depose Torrijos was also largely foiled by Noriega.

In recognition of his devotion, Noriega was elevated to the rank of lieutenant colonel and appointed head of military intelligence, a role in which he forged ties with the United States intelligence community. Persistent allegations of his participation in drug trafficking tainted his cooperation to the Nixon administration, which included assisting to secure the release of two American freighter crews from Havana. By the late 1970s, Noriega had become the most dreaded man in Panama, thanks to his reputation as head of the country's intelligence agency and his penchant for using harassment and threats against opposition organisations and their leaders. Following Torrijos's 1981 death in an aircraft accident, Noriega competed with other civilian and military leaders for control. He became general in 1983 after succeeding to the National Guard leadership, which he used to unite the military forces into the Panamanian Defence Forces.

In the mid-1980s, allegations surrounding the heinous and cruel killing of Hugo Spadafora, an outspoken opponent, led to the escalation of charges against Noriega. With the impending power transfer outlined in the Panama Canal Treaty, tensions with the United States government were certain to rise as more proof of drug money laundering and the sale of banned American technology and information surfaced. Noriega sought to govern via a puppet government in 1989 after cancelling the presidential elections. The United States invaded Panama as part of Operation Just Cause after a failed military coup d'état against Manuel Noriega. He was granted asylum at the Vatican nunciature (embassy) in Panama City and stayed there for ten days while a psychological warfare squad from the United States Army played rock music inside. Upon his eventual surrender to U.S. authorities on January 3, 1990, Noriega was taken to Miami for his arraignment on several criminal counts.

The United States federal court in 1992 found Noriega guilty of money laundering, racketeering, and cocaine trafficking. Although he first got a 40-year sentence, it was subsequently reduced. On September 9, 2007, Noriega finished out the remainder of his sentence, which lasted for around 17 years. He was convicted of money laundering and other offences in 1999 when he was prosecuted in absentia in France, but he stayed in jail while he challenged his extradition. After his 2010 appeal was denied by the United States Supreme Court, Noriega was extradited to France in April and stood trial in June. He received a seven-year jail term the month after his conviction. Noriega was convicted for the murder of political opponents, including Spadafora, in absentia at his trial in Panama in 2011, but France consented to extradite him. Noriega started serving three 20-year jail sentences upon his return to his own country on December 11, 2011.

# 97.

# KING DAVID (ISRAEL)

The second king of the ancient Israelite and Judaic kingdom, David (flourished about 1000 BCE). He unified the Israelite tribes under one ruler and established the Judaean dynasty. After David died, his son Solomon continued his father's kingdom expansion. Judaism, Christianity, and Islam all hold David in high esteem.

Paris Psalter (Gr. 139), miniature of David writing psalms, dating to the 10th century; housed in the Bibliothèque Nationale, Paris. 26.0 by 35.9 centimetres.

Several chapters in the Hebrew Bible's books of Samuel (Old Testament) 1 and 2 provide the main evidence for David's career. Because of his extraordinary talent as a hymn writer, harpist, and poet, he is also said to have composed many of the psalms. The lack of tangible proof of his rule is a contentious issue among historians. There are academics who claim to have found evidence that supports the biblical narrative of David's reign. Some argue that the evidence from the archaeological record shows that David was more of a talented tribal leader in a pastoral lifestyle than the monarch of a growing kingdom. Even though it was inscribed almost a century after the conventional date of his rule, not all academics accept a piece from a stone stela that mentions the "house of David" (a reference to his political dynasty). The biblical narrative of David's rule is the primary source for the information presented in this page.

David, the youngest son of a man from Bethlehem named Jesse, began his career as an attendant in the court of Saul, the first king of Israel, after serving as a shepherd for his father, as recorded in 1 Samuel. The brothers of David fought with King Saul in Israel's war against the Philistines, who lived in the adjacent territory. In order to provide his brothers with food and supplies, young David would often return to the camp. In 1 Samuel 17, the giant Goliath, who was armed to the teeth, issued a 40-day challenge to Saul, daring him to send an army to confront him. Nobody dared to confront this fierce fighter until David stepped forward, prepared with nothing but a sling and some stones. The giant was slain when David struck him on the forehead with a stone. Saul was envious of his rising stardom as a warrior since he kept standing out in the conflicts with the Philistines. A conspiracy to assassinate David was devised by Saul in his fear that the people would anoint him king. David, aided by his faithful companion Jonathan, the oldest son of Saul, escaped to the coastal plain of Palestine in southern Judah and Philistia. It was there that he started to establish the groundwork for his career, demonstrating remarkable wisdom and insight.

David, a wanted bandit in Judah (south of the Levant), lived the life of a Robin Hood on the boundary of his tribe territory in the desert. At first antagonistic towards the locals, he eventually warmed up to them as a leader and organiser of a gang of exiles and bandits who gradually restored stolen goods and protected the populace against future raids. Despite being anointed by the prophet Samuel to be Israel's future king (1 Samuel 16), David's deeds while in exile helped secure his coronation as the rightful heir to Saul's throne after the deaths of Saul and Jonathan at the hands of the Philistines on Mount Gilboa.

# 98.

# GIUSEPPE GARIBALDI (ITALY)

Italian patriot and soldier of the Risorgimento, Giuseppe Garibaldi was born July 4, 1807, in Nice, French Empire (now in France). He died June 2, 1882, in Caprera, Italy. Garibaldi was a republican who helped bring Italy together under the Savoy royal house by leading the guerrilla Redshirts to victory in Sicily and Naples.

In addition to spending almost a decade at sea, Garibaldi was born into a family of coastal merchants and fishermen. In 1832, he became a merchant captain with a master's certificate. He was influenced by the famous Italian nationalist Giuseppe Mazzini and the French socialist thinker the comte de Saint-Simon by the time he served in the navy of the kingdom of Piedmont-Sardinia in 1833 and 1834. After participating in a mutiny in 1834 that aimed to spark a republican revolution in Piedmont, Garibaldi fled to France and was later executed by a court in Genoa while he was away.

During his exile in South America from 1836 to 1848, Garibaldi was deeply affected by the revolutionary and turbulent years that unfolded on that continent. During the little republic of Rio Grande do Sul's failed effort to break away from the Brazilian Empire, he offered to serve as its navy commander. In reality, his main activity was to target Brazilian shipping companies. Through a series of daring land and sea adventures, he was able to elope with a married lady named Anna Maria Ribeiro da Silva (Anita), who fought by his side until she died. Garibaldi opted to resign from his position with Rio Grande after a string of Brazilian wins in 1839–1840. Along with Anita and their kid, he drove a herd of cattle on the lengthy journey to Montevideo. Unfortunately, he was unable to adjust to civilian life despite his best efforts as a teacher and business traveller. He led the Uruguayan fleet in the 1842 liberation struggle, this time against Argentina's tyrant Juan Manuel de Rosas. The next year, while still serving Uruguay, Garibaldi became famous for his association with the Redshirts when he assumed leadership of a newly established Italian Legion in Montevideo. Italy awarded him a sword of honour, funded by contributions, as his name spread throughout Europe after his tiny but courageous action at the Battle of Sant'Antonio in 1846.

He first caught the eye of Alexandre Dumas père, who would go on to do much to promote his fame, when he was temporarily in command of the defence of Montevideo in 1847. Other outsiders were also pleased by Garibaldi's character as an honest and competent guy. He obtained priceless knowledge of guerilla tactics during his time in South America, which he subsequently put to excellent use against unprepared French and Austrian forces. These early acts of resistance shaped him into a career rebel, an unyielding individualist who, throughout his life, maintained his pampas gaucho attire and acted as if fighting for freedom were constant realities.

# 99.

# SUN YAT-SEN (CHINA)

Sun Yat-sen, the founding father of modern China, was a prominent figure in Chinese history. He was born on November 12, 1866, in Xiangshan (now Zhongshan), Guangdong province, China, and died on March 12, 1925, in Beijing. Sun was the head of the Chinese Nationalist Party, or Kuomintang (Pinyin: Guomindang). In addition to being a key figure in the 1911–12 revolution that deposed the Qing (Manchu) dynasty, he was the Republic of China's first interim president (1911–12) and de facto ruler (1923–25).

Xiangshan, a province in Guangdong, South China, is where Sun was born into a poor farming family. Sun Mei, his labourer brother, had already come to Hawaii in 1879 and brought him to Honolulu, where he spent three years at a British missionary school and another year at Oahu College, an American institution, where he first encountered Western ideas. Sun travelled back to his home town in 1883 when his brother disapproved of his Christian leanings; that autumn, he enrolled in the Diocesan Home in Hong

Kong for further study; and same year, he was baptised by an American missionary.

His parents picked his wife, Lu Muzhen (1867-1952), and he married her in 1884 when he was a student at Queen's College (formerly the Government Central School). This union resulted in the birth of a boy and two daughters. The next year, in 1886, he returned to Hawaii and enrolled in the medical school at the Guangzhou (Canton) Hospital. After a while, he changed schools and earned a degree in 1892 from Hong Kong's College of Medicine for Chinese.

Despite Sun's lack of formal political training, his ambitions were unquenchable, and he couldn't help but be bothered by the humiliation endured by China as a result of its adherence to ancient practises under the restrictive Qing era. With the hope of better political fortunes in the north, he left his medical practise in Guangzhou in 1894. He laid forth his plans for China's strengthening in a lengthy letter to Li Hongzhang, governor-general of Zhili (Chihli, now Hebei) province, but Li only gave him a cursory approval of his agricultural-sericultural partnership. In October 1894, Sun travelled to Hawaii with this very little information and established the Revive China Society (Xingzhonghui), the precursor to the clandestine revolutionary forces he would eventually lead. From what we can tell, the whole membership consisted of lower-class Guangdong residents, including clerks, peasants, and craftsmen.

# 100.

# MOBUTU SESE SEKO (ZAIRE)

Born on October 14, 1930, in Lisala, Belgian Congo (now the Democratic Republic of the Congo), Mobutu Sese Seko was president of Zaire (now the Democratic Republic of the Congo) from 1965 until his ouster in 1997 due to a rebellion. He ruled for about 32 years.

Originating from a background in missionary education, Mobutu embarked on his military career in the Belgian Congolese Force Publique in 1949, where he worked his way up from the ranks of clerk to sergeant major—the highest position available to Africans at the time. During his time in the army, Mobutu wrote for newspapers in Léopoldville, which is now Kinshasa. His career took off when he was discharged in 1956; he worked his way up to editor of the monthly Actualités Africaines and then correspondent for the daily L'Avenir ("The Future").

In 1958, Mobutu joined the newly formed Congolese National Movement (Mouvement National Congolais; MNC), which he had met via his press ties with Patrice Lumumba, a nationalist leader in the

Congo. Until Lumumba was released from prison for his nationalist activities in the Congo, Mobutu represented him at the Brussels Round Table Conference on Congo independence in 1960. During the meeting, Mobutu voiced his support for Lumumba's (and ultimately accepted) plans to establish a highly centralised government in the newly independent Congo.

Mobutu was named secretary of state for national defence by the coalition administration of President Joseph Kasavubu and Premier Lumumba upon the Congo's independence on June 30, 1960. After eight days, the Belgian officers in charge of the Congo's Force Publique were overthrown in a mutiny. Mobutu could have an impact on the escalating power struggle between Lumumba and Kasavubu since he was one of the few commanders with any authority over the army, which he had obtained by generously paying the mutineers' commissions and back pay.

Subtly, Mobutu backed Kasavubu's effort to fire Lumumba. In September 1960, when Lumumba gathered his troops to depose Kasavubu, Mobutu declared himself the leader of the country and said that he was "neutralising" all politicians. But Mobutu deposed Kasavubu as president in February 1961 and appointed Mobutu head of the military. It is widely thought that Congolese or Katangese forces assassinated Lumumba after he was detained by Mobutu's forces and sent to Katanga. Many also hold Mobutu partially responsible for Lumumba's killing.

In his role as chief commander, Mobutu restructured the armed forces. President Kasavubu and his minister, Moise Tshombe, were embroiled in a power struggle in 1965, which led to Mobutu's coup d'état and assumption of the president. A coup d'état orchestrated by white mercenaries stationed in the Congolese army was quenched two years later by Mobutu. Among his policies aimed at reviving the Congolese economy were calls for international investment and the nationalisation of the Katanga copper mines. Imports of food became more necessary as a result of the delayed agricultural regeneration.

Africaized names were one of Mobutu's policies as president. After changing its name from the Democratic Republic of the Congo (Congo [Kinshasa]) to the Republic of Zaire in October 1971, the nation went back to its original name in 1997. He went by Mobutu Sese Seko in January 1972 instead of Joseph-Désiré Mobutu. "The all-powerful warrior who, due to his endurance and inflexible will to win, will go from conquest to conquest, leaving fire in his wake"—Koko Ngbendu Wa Za Banga.

By appointing civilians to high-ranking government positions, Mobutu sought to downplay the regime's military character. Up until 1990, his Popular Movement of the Revolution (MPR) was the only legitimate political party in the nation, and he used it to rally the people. Some university students, small farmers who did not benefit from the economic restoration effort, ethnic groupings that had played pivotal roles in earlier administrations, and a large number of Congolese refugees were among those who opposed his authority. In addition, Mobutu was always on edge because Katangese rebels in Angola posed a danger of attacking the Shaba region, which was Mobutu's Africanized term for the Katanga province.

After the Katangese, supported by Angola, invaded Zaire in 1977, Mobutu asked the French for military help to save the country. Two one-man campaigns, in 1970 and 1977, brought him another term as president. Although Mobutu was skilled at preserving his reign through several coup attempts and internal uprisings, his government was unable to create the favourable circumstances for economic expansion and prosperity. The country's infrastructure deteriorated due to Mobutu's alleged accumulation of one of the world's greatest personal fortunes and pervasive government corruption, inefficiency, and neglect.

As the Cold War drew to a close in the 1990s, Mobutu saw a significant decline in the financial aid he had received from Western countries in exchange for his interference in neighbouring Zaire's internal affairs. Because of his illness and marginalisation within the multiparty system, Mobutu ultimately handed over power to rebel leader Laurent Kabila in May 1997. Kabila's soldiers had started taking power seven months earlier. Soon after, Mobutu passed away while living in exile.

*****